Go Programming

John P. Baugh

ISBN: 1453636676
EAN-13: 9781453636671

TABLE OF CONTENTS

What is This Book About and Who is It For?

This book introduces a new, open source, concurrent, garbage collected, experimental systems programming language called Go. Go was invented by developers at Google and is intended to offer faster development, better support for modern computing technologies, and cleaner code than other systems languages. And perhaps most importantly, Go provides a "fresh start", if you will, for developers.

While Go is described as primarily being a systems language, it is, like C or C++, fully capable of supporting the development of front end applications.

Go is currently only available for Linux and Mac platforms, but if you are a Windows user - don't fret! In this book, I explain the options you currently have, including usage of a virtual machine, and I will even show you how to easily install Ubuntu(a popular Linux OS) for dual booting with your Windows Machine with very little hassle!

However, at the time of this writing, there has been significant effort by several volunteers at creating a port to work with MinGW to enable Windows users to develop in Go. By the time you get this book, there *may* be something significant and usable, so check the official website at *http://www.golang.org* first and see if there are any compilers for MinGW available.

Because Go is new and open source, it offers a lot of potential for us, the developers. It gives us the ability to help shape it to our needs and desires. Because many other programming languages (such as C, C++, and Java) were invented over a decade ago (some even two decades ago or longer), they weren't invented with modern computing technologies in mind.

Go changes the game with built-in, excellent support for many modern technologies like communication channels and concurrency, as well as several coding standards enforced by the compiler to help you keep your code as clean and efficient as possible... not to mention a built-in type to make unit testing quick and easy!

In this book, I assume you have some experience with a high level programming language like C, C++, C#, Java, Objective C, Python, Ruby, or others. I do not expect you to be an expert programmer, but more experienced programmers will most likely gain a deeper understanding of the Go language than less experienced programmers, at least at first. However, this book is perfectly readable and understandable for someone who has a fundamental understanding of a high level language, but not a ton of years experience under his/her belt. I spend some time on the primitives of the language, and throughout the entire book, I teach by tutorial and example, with details where necessary

Visit this book's website for errata, updates, and other useful information at:

http://www.goprogrammingbook.com

About the Author

John P. Baugh has been developing software in various forms for over ten years. He holds a Master of Science Degree in Computer Science from the University of Michigan at Dearborn. He is currently preparing to pursue his Ph.D in Information Systems Engineering.

He is an Adjunct Lecturer of Computer Science at the University of Michigan at Dearborn, and has taught at Schoolcraft College in Livonia, Michigan as well. He has taught classes ranging from beginning computer science to intermediate computer science with C++, Java programming, as well as a course in C# programming with an emphasis on game design.

John also currently works in Ann Arbor, Michigan for Siemens PLM Software as a software engineer in the Licensing and Business Intelligence Group, writing and maintaining licensing software for various products.

Prior to working for Siemens PLM Software, John was a Research Assistant in the Vehicular Networking Systems Research Laboratory at the University of Michigan-Dearborn.

For more information about the Go Programming language, other languages, and other information on the author and his availability for book and article writing, or consulting, please visit his personal sites at:

http://www.jpbaugh.com

http://www.goprogrammingbook.com

Chapter 1

Introduction to Go

One day in particular, a few months ago, I was in my room at my house doing some development using C++. It was a rather large program, so being the experienced developer that I am, I did what every true-blooded geek would do in this situation... I hit the "Build" button in my IDE of choice, and walked out of my room to go make myself a sandwich and pour myself a soda (whose name shall remain secret, but if you're interested, it is a popular black liquid and doesn't rhyme with "poke".) I was reasonably quick about it, and when I returned to my room, the compilation and linking was just finishing up.

Most of the seasoned developers are reading this and thinking, "Umm... so what's your point?". The point is that I didn't think anything of leaving the room for a few minutes while I waited for this program to compile and link. In fact, I do this quite frequently. I do this at work with my very fast and powerful dual core processor computer, as well as at home on one of my somewhat dinosaurian personal desktop. So, the bottom line is - development takes a long time with many of the languages and development environments we use. Granted, it's nice to leave the room to get a sandwich and a soda once in a while. But when I'm not hungry or thirsty, I certainly don't like sitting around waiting! Well... neither did the inventors of the Go language.

1.1   Why a New Language?

The story goes something like this. One day, some of the developers at Google were talking about this and that, and had an idea. They originally wanted to write some efficient libraries to improve support for various modern computing paradigms, and expand a language like C++ or Java. But then they started to think... writing more libraries for already bloated languages with no built-in support for modern computing paradigms was not the solution. In fact, it seemed to them like it was going in the wrong direction.

"Why can't I have good support for communication channels? Or concurrency, without having to deal too much with cross-thread resource contention and other things that make me want to pull my hair out?!"

These questions, and several others, prompted some developers at Google to invent the Go programming language. The inventors of Go were tired with having to always choose between ease in development of a program, and the execution and/or compilation efficiency of the program. They dared to ask the question, "Why can't we have *everything*?" Go is intended to provide easy and fast development, quick compilation, and efficient and fast executables.

1.2   How Does Go Compare with C++?

Go is unquestionably a high level language, just like C, C++, or Java. However, it differs greatly with languages like C, C++, and Java. In this section, we'll take a look at a few similarities and differences between Go and C/C++. This section will be of greatest benefit to those who are familiar with C, C++, and/or Java. It is by no means exhaustive, but may provide insight into how Go and C++ differ, and how they are similar.

1.2.1   Functions

Both Go and C++ have concepts of "functions" though they are slightly different between the languages.

In C/C++ for example, when someone is referring to a *function*, they are typically referring to a body of code (a series of steps) with a name (identifier), a return type, and parameters. Additionally, when one refers to a function within a class, it is referred to as a *member function*, or sometimes a *method*.

Here's an example of a basic function in C/C++, to perform squaring of an integer:

```
int Square(int n)
{
      return n * n;
}
```

And here's that same function in Go:

```
func Square(n int) int{
      return n * n
}
```

Notice the differences and similarities between the two languages. In C/C++, the return type is specified at the very front of the function definition. Then the identifier, then the parameter list, then the body of the function.

In the Go example of the same Squaring algorithm, notice a couple key differences from the C/C++ code. Firstly, the `func` keyword declares that there is a function about to be defined. Then, the identifier, the parameter list, and at the *end* of the function header, the return type (`int`).

There are many other interesting aspects of functions with Go (including the ability to return and assign multiple values with a single call), but I hope this will give a basic idea of some of the syntax.

Later in this book, we'll delve deeper into some of the more interesting aspects of Go functions, and we're *definitely* going to save Go methods (special functions with a receiver) for later.

Go is somewhat like the first cat you've ever had contact with, when the only animals you've ever owned were dogs. You go to pet the cat in all the usual "dog places", and it slices your hand open with its incredibly fast, sharp claws, and hisses at you. Well... to be honest, Go is a lot nicer than this, but you get the point - you don't know where to "pet" Go yet, so just take it nice and easy.

By the way. True story. Be careful around cats.

1.2.2   *Is Go Object Oriented like C++?*

This is a tricky question. In the classical sense of providing full encapsulation, inheritance, and polymorphism, no. But Go does have many object oriented features.

Go does not support inheritance at all. We will see later how Go implements *interfaces* and allows for "pseudo-inheritance". It is quite different from the way it is done in C++ and will take quite a bit of explanation. Just be patient. Go also allows for types to contain other types in way that allows the types to take on somewhat of a superclass/subclass relationship, but it isn't *quite* the same as it is in C++.

There is a method (not in the programming sense of the word) to the madness, though. Type hierarchies cause a lot of overhead with compilation, and multiple inheritance in languages like C++ is even worse. The inventors of Go found complete object orientation to be quite cumbersome and that it causes compilation to take a long time with generation of symbol tables, the establishment of relationships between objects in type hierarchies and other problems endemic in this type of code. This is why they opted out of a completely object oriented world and found a middle ground where they hope the OOP lovers out there will be content.

Many programmers who are staunch about object oriented development (like myself) may be looking at this as a step back. But it's actually not. I can tell you honestly, as a developer who is very fond of strict object orientation in my C++ and Java code, that Go's way of doing things is not a move back to the entirely functional programming paradigm of the Dark Ages, or anything of the sort. In fact, it's quite a relevant and modern approach, which we will see later.

In summary, Go provides a clean way that supports an object oriented style of programming without all the confusion and clutter. When you get to the part of this book about interfaces and see how Go actually *does* things, you'll probably like it a lot. Trust me!

1.2.3 How do I free memory in Go?

Memory cleanup in Go is more akin to Java than C++. Go has automatic garbage collection. So, you don't have to (and in fact, can't) explicitly use `delete` or `free()` to free memory allocated to various variables.

At the time of this writing, the developers working on Go were exploring options to make the garbage collection much more efficient. The current build of Go utilizes a simple *mark and sweep* method of garbage collection.

1.2.4   Other stuff to be aware of

There are many significant differences between Go and C++. Some require much more explanation than the brief overview we provide in this section. Much of the nitty gritty of the Go language will be examined as we explore the language throughout this book.

Here are just a few things to be aware of as you read through the book:

- The syntax of Go may be very different from what you expect. For example, the order of the data type, identifier, and parameter list may not be what you expect.

- Go allows multiple return values from functions and methods. This leads to some unusual syntax that you may not recognize or be able to follow until you see some good solid examples later in the book.

- Go has interfaces, but they are not what you'd expect if you've dealt with languages like Java.

- Go does not allow coercion (implicit type casting). If you try to coerce one type to another, it is a compiler error. You must explicitly tell Go when you're switching between types.

- There is no pointer arithmetic. Pointer arithmetic leads to a lot of misbehaving code and erroneous memory access, including fatal crashes of software, so Go removed this capability entirely.

- Strings are immutable. You cannot create a string and change one of the characters in it.

- Identifiers in Go are in Unicode. So you may see special characters, such as those in Chinese, Hebrew or Arabic as identifiers. However, you can't mix character sets.

- Capitalization of identifiers, as we shall see later, has an impact on the visibility of the identifier (capital letters mean public, lower case means private)

- There is no operator overloading in Go.

- There is no function overloading in Go. This avoids the language fragility caused by functions with the same name and different signatures, and doesn't cause a mess with things like the ugly "name mangling" that happens in C++.

1.3   Summary

In this chapter, we briefly explored the Go programming language. We saw why the inventors of Go thought it was necessary to start over with a fresh, new systems programming language instead of just working with older languages like C/C++ or Java.

We saw some similarities and differences between C++ and the Go programming language. It is possible to program Go in an object-oriented fashion, but Go does not support strict object hierarchy, full encapsulation, or polymorphism like C++ does.

We also took a brief tour of what Go does in terms of garbage collection. Within that subsection, we saw that you don't need to `delete` or `free()` allocated memory, and in fact, you cannot explicitly do so. Go takes care of the garbage collection itself.

And finally, we looked at several differences and "gotcha" issues that programmers coming from another language may find interesting or unusual.

In the next chapter, we'll take a look at how to install Go and any necessary supporting software, including virtual machines, or dual boots for those who have Windows boxes.

Chapter 2

Installing Go and Other Support Software

Most of the necessary instructions to installing Go onto your Linux or Macintosh box are available at the official Go website (*http://www.golang.org*). However, in this chapter I will provide some useful information to get you up and running.

2.1   What Platforms can I install Go on?

As of the time of this writing, there are two officially supported operating systems (or system groups):

- Linux
- Macintosh OS X

And, there are three processor architectures supported:

- x86_64 (also known as the amd64 instruction set. Don't be fooled by the name! This is for *both* Intel 64, and AMD 64.)
- x86_32 (also known as the x86 or 386. These are, as the name suggests, 32 bit processors.)

- ARM (These are processors with a 32 bit RISC instruction set. This particular port is not fully complete, and does have some bugs in at as of this writing)

In my opinion, the best port is <insert favorite flavor of Linux> on the x86_64 processor. Because a lot of Linux users are very passionate about open source solutions, it is also likely that they will ensure Go is well tested on Linux. The x86_32 is, according to the official website, not as "well soaked", which indicates it hasn't been as thoroughly tested, but they believe it should be as solid.

And, as far as Macintosh users are concerned - you must have OS X running on an Intel 64 machine. Since, to the best of my knowledge, Macintosh OS X has never run on any 32 bit Intel processors, the x86_32 is not even applicable to Macintosh users.

2.2 But what if I'm a Windows user?

Whatever anyone feels about Windows, there is no doubt it has a healthy majority of the market as far as personal computer is concerned. In fact, as much as Linux users want to deny the facts, a large portion of companies use Visual Studio on Windows machines to do their primary development. So, while Go has been geared toward the Linux and Macintosh users, there are still very good options available for Windows users!

I will describe a couple options for individuals with Windows PCs. And they are both free! And, as always, you do have the option of going through the trouble of partitioning your hard drive and putting a full install of your favorite Linux OS, but this will not be covered here. It is also important to note that as of this writing, there is a project going on to port Go to work with MinGW on Windows. So check the official site often to see if they've developed a port that works for you.

2.2.1   *Virtual Machine*

One option for Windows users who want to have access to a Linux box, for example, but don't want to invest in new hardware and install Linux is a *virtual machine*. We're not talking about the JVM (Java Virtual Machine), although there are similarities conceptually.

Basically, a virtual machine emulates hardware, and runs *virtual appliances* on this "hardware". For example, if you wanted to install Red Hat, Ubuntu, or Suse Linux on your virtual machine, you'd just download the virtual appliance for that particular operating system, and install in onto your virtual machine as if the virtual machine were an actual piece of hardware.

And while I won't provide a complete step by step installation for this particular technique, I'll give you some basic steps as resources to quickly get you going if you choose this option. In my opinion, one of the best virtual machines available for Windows is VMware Player. So to get started:

1.   Go to ***http://www.vmware.com***
2.   Go to *Support & Downloads*
3.   Click on *VMware Player* under *Desktop Products*, listed on the page
4.   Download and install the VMware Player

Then, you'll need a Linux virtual machine appliance to run on your VMware Player.

Note: If you plan on running a 64 bit virtual machine appliance, the *actual* hardware on your physical machine (your computer) needs to be 64 bit.

5.   Now, go to *Virtual Appliances* near the top of the page
6.   Do a search for your virtual appliance of choice, such as "Linux", "Red Hat", "Suse", or "Ubuntu"
7.   Follow the instructions to download and install the virtual appliance of your choice.

After you've installed the virtual appliance, you should be able to treat it as if it were an actual Linux box. This means you can install Go and whatever else you might need!

2.2.2   Dual Booting with Ubuntu

Personally, this is my favorite option. I have a system that dual boots with Windows 7 and Ubuntu.

Ubuntu is one of my favorite Linux operating systems. I've dealt with many different operating systems based on the Linux kernel, and Ubuntu is by far my favorite for several different reasons.

I like Linux. Don't get me wrong. In fact, I love Linux. But, a lot of Linux users (many of whom are involved in the development of their particular Linux of choice) *hate* Windows. And, albeit a rogue element of the Linux community, some even hate Windows so much, that they hate Windows users.

Ubuntu isn't like that. Ubuntu is a very Windows friendly community. And in fact, they provide one of the easiest dual boot installers I've ever seen for a Linux OS. This magical little jewel is called *Wubi*.

Now, here are some notes before you being. This installer is *not* going to partition your hard drive. It actually cleverly creates a special file that Linux recognizes as a hard drive. Then, it modifies some of your boot settings so that when your computer boots, it will let you select either your Windows OS or the Ubuntu installation.

Wubi is *not* itself a Linux port. It is simply an installer of Linux for Windows users. (**W**indows **UB**untu **I**nstaller. Clever, eh?) And the version of Ubuntu that installed is a legitimate, complete installation of Ubuntu. It is not a virtual machine.

I've used this installer before, and although I do have access to other Linux machines, I decided I wanted Ubuntu on my laptop. I have had very little trouble with it. Windows 7 and Ubuntu play nicely together.

Before we beigin, there are a few important notes about installing with Wubi:

1.   Hard drive read/writes are a wee bit slower, but shouldn't affect your Go programming significantly unless your computer is a complete dinosaur.

2.   Wubi does not support hibernation. The details are available on the official website.

3.   The Wubi-installed Ubuntu is significantly more sensitive than an installation on a partition would be, to

power offs. If you shut the power off while Ubuntu is doing something, you may completely destroy the Ubuntu installation and have to start from scratch. If it doesn't destroy the installation completely, it may cause strange malfunctions like large sea creatures jumping out of your machine and making a mess of your room (*Wubi on Whales*? Okay, I had to. Moving on...)

Regardless, your Windows machine should be safe, as Wubi is not really messing much with your actual hardware or doing partitioning or anything. But, use caution.

So here is where you go to get Wubi:

http://www.wubi-installer.org

It's very simple. Just download it, and follow the installation instructions as you would with any product. Then, you will restart your machine, and be able to select the OS of your choice with the arrow keys. *Voila!*

2.3 Installing Go

Okay, so you've got the appropriate hardware and OS, now how do you actually install Go?

In this section, I'm going to focus on installing Go onto Ubuntu, but most of the installation should be similar regardless of what type of Linux (or Mac) you have. As long as it's a *Unix-like* OS, you can use Unix commands, so you should be in business.

The official installation guide is on the official website, located at:

http://www.golang.org/doc/install.html

I recommend opening up this webpage and using it as your primary guide through installation. However, I will make some important notes about the installation that could throw you off, especially if you're not familiar with Unix-based systems.

2.3.1   Environment Variables

These are *crucial* to your installation. You should edit the .bashrc file, as prescribed on the official installation page. The .bashrc file is basically a settings file, so that when you open a terminal window, all of the necessary environment variables and prerequisites are set up.

If you don't edit this file, you'd need to do manual exports of all the environment variables every time you opened up a terminal window. That is no fun at all. Note also that the .bashrc is not visible when you simple do an `ls` (list) command. In order to see if it's there or not, you can do `ls -a` (list all) command.

So, in the .bashrc, you must write the following:

```
export GOROOT=$HOME/go
export GOARCH=amd64
export GOOS=linux
export GOBIN=$HOME/bin
```

Make sure to save the .bashrc file with these exports. Then, close the terminal window, and open a new one. Then, do an

```
env | grep '^GO'
```

to ensure that the GO environment variables have been added to your environment. Alternatively, you can do an

`echo $GOROOT` (or $GO<whatever>)

to make sure the variables are there.

Now, there is one more thing related to environment variables that you have to do that is very important. The official installation page says that the environment variable `GOBIN` is optional, but I found that my installation did not work appropriately without it. If you don't export `GOBIN` and *also* add it to your `PATH`, the installation may have problems when it gets to the tests at the end.

To add the `GOBIN` (where your Go compiler and linker reside) to your `PATH`, do the following:

`export PATH=$GOBIN:$PATH`

This will take your new `GOBIN` environment variable, and append it to the front of your `PATH` environment variable.

As a note, if you have any difficulties or warnings about missing directories, you make have to create a directory (with `mkdir`, for example) that is missing.

2.3.2   *Installing Mercurial*

Mercurial is a revision control application that allows projects (like Go) to maintain repositories with the latest version of their software, so that you can easily download it and upgrade your installation.

In order to test and see if you have mercurial installed, type

24

```
hg
```

in a terminal window.

If it says it doesn't exist, or hasn't been installed yet, first, try using the options for installation that are given.

I personally found that the method provided for Ubuntu on the official site did not work. So I went directly to Mercurial's download page:

http://mercurial.selenic.com/wiki/Download

Then, I went to the *Linux (.deb)* section for my Ubuntu OS (obviously, you should go to the Linux installation that you have).

Then, I selected Karmic (which is the version of Ubuntu I have), and it takes you to the download page.

The actual download link will be at the bottom (labeled amd64 or i386). Select the appropriate processor architecture for your platform, and then a mirror site to download it from.

I personally opened mine with GDebi Package Installer, which is an incredibly helpful installation tool.

Since Mercurial has dependencies (which include things like Python), you may have to install these dependencies first.

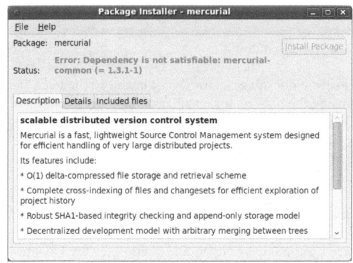

Figure 2.3.2-1

If you try to install the mercurial package, you will likely get the error in *Figure 2.3.2-1*.

If you get an error like this one, just install the dependency that is listed in the error, and it should take care of the problem.

I found that *all* I really needed to install was the dependency of mercurial, listed as **mercurial-common (= 1.3.1-1)**, and nothing else.

Then I did a

```
sudo apt-get install mercurial
```

That was enough to get the hg command working. Your experience with Linux or Macintosh may be slightly different than my experience, so you may have to play around with what dependencies need downloaded. But the overall installation should be fairly straightforward.

2.3.3　　Fetching the Go Repository

Once you have mercurial installed, you can fetch the Go repository:

```
hg clone -r release https://go.googlecode.com/hg/
$GOROOT
```

You must make *sure* that $GOROOT doesn't exist yet, or at very least, that it is empty.

2.3.4　　Installing Go

Once you have all the supporting software installed, it is pretty simple to install Go. Per the official installation page, you must ensure you have the following applications installed:

- Bison (a parser generator)
- Gcc
- Libc6-dev
- Ed
- Gawk
- Make

To install these, you type:

```
sudo apt-get install bison gcc libc6-dev ed gawk make
```

This should take care of the installations of the final support software. Note carefully that the above syntax will work on Debian-based Linux systems like Ubuntu. For most other Linux distributions, RPMs will be used.

Now, to build Go, we follow the steps from the official installation site:

```
cd $GOROOT/src
./all.bash
```

When it finishes building, you should get something like:

```
0 known bugs; 0 unexpected bugs
```

although the number of known bugs could vary.

2.4   Compiling, Linking, and Running

By this point, you should have Go installed. This section will hopefully help you to ensure everything's working correctly by taking the compiler and linker for a test drive.

Go has some strange names for its official compilers and linkers. These will vary from platform to platform.

The following shows you the name of the compiler and linker for your platform:

Platform	Compiler	Linker
X86_64	6g	6l
X86_32	8g	8l
ARM	5g	5l

Note that, for the linkers, the second character is a lowercase "L" for "linker", not the number 1.

The entire process of creating an executable with Go is as follows:

```
$ 6g filename.go
```

```
$ 6l filename.6
$ ./6.out
```

Notice, the 6 would be replaced with the appropriate number based on what platform you are on. Also, note the $ signs appear at the beginning of basic prompts in the bash shell, and are not part of the commands themselves.

Also note that you can (optionally) change the name of the executable that is output, by using the -o flag:

```
$ 6g filename.go
$ 6l -o myExeName filename.6
$ ./myExeName
```

where myExeName is the name you want your executable file to have.

The Go compiler is known as gc, for "Go Compiler" (imagine that!). It should not be confused with gcc, or gccgo.

2.4.1   What About gccgo?

If you don't want to use the Go compilers provided by the inventors/developers at Google, you have another option. gccgo is a compiler frontend for gcc, which as most of the readers probably know, is the very popular GNU compiler.

The gccgo typically compiles slower than the (6g, 8g, 5g) compiler, but the generated executable is a little bit faster.

For more information about the installation of gccgo, please refer to:

http://golang.org/doc/gccgo_install.html

It is also important to note that, although much of this is outside the scope of this book, gccgo currently offers some interoperability with C. As with much of the projects related to Go, much of the specifics are subject to change.

2.5   Summary

In this chapter, we covered a lot of territory related to the installation of Go and supporting software.

Go is officially supported on Linux and Macintosh. However, Windows users still have options, including using a virtual machine, or Wubi, a handy installer of Ubuntu so that you can dual boot with Windows and Ubuntu Linux. These two options are described in a reasonable amount of detail. A third option is to do a partition, and full installation of your Linux (or potentially MacOS) of choice. This option is only mentioned, and is not described in detail. Furthermore, a MinGW port is in the works as of the time of this writing, and it is quite likely you will be able to program in Go even more easily on Windows.

After ensuring we have the correct hardware and/or software to install Go, we set up the necessary environment variables. Next, we explored how to install Mercurial, a revision control management system that allows us to install Go. I described some of the pitfalls and issues you may have when you try to install Mercurial, including potential problems with dependencies.

Then, we learned how to fetch the code for Go from the Go repository. And finally, we installed Go itself, so that we could compile and link applications with the 6g (or 8g or

5g, depending on your platform) compiler, and the 6l (or 8l, or 5l) linker.

Finally, I mentioned gccgo, the frontend for the popular GNU GCC compiler. It is a separate project from the official Go project at Google, but was designed based on the language specification and works almost as well as the Google Go compilers. Also of importance is that it compiles more slowly than the Google Go compilers (6g, 8g, or 5g) but that the executable is often slightly faster.

In the next chapter, now that we have a basic history and motivation under our belt and the appropriate software installed, we will begin learning about how to program in Go.

Chapter 3

Getting Started with Go Programming

Hopefully the previous chapters were not too mind numbing. I tried to give you a basic understanding of why we should even be interested in Go as a language. Also, when I start out with a new programming language, I often find installation to be one of the most irritating aspects of the whole process, so I tried to keep my installation instructions to a bare minimum, but provide enough information so that you can install Go with very little trouble.

Anyway, enough of the dark and dirty past - let's get to the fun, shall we? In this chapter, we'll get into the nitty gritty of the basics. We'll learn a lot about the syntax of Go, the different data types that are available, basic I/O, keywords, operators, and a whole boatload of other useful information. I'll provide some good, clear, and concise examples so that you'll gain a solid understanding of what is actually going on.

3.1   Standard I/O

In this section, we'll go over some basic mechanisms for printing to the console, and retrieving input from the keyboard.

3.1.1 The Obligatory "Hello World"

In this subsection, we're going to use the `fmt` package to do simple output to the console, in a fashion similar to what you may be familiar with in C.

```
1   package main
2   import "fmt"
3
4   func main(){
5       fmt.Printf("Hi there!\n ");
6   }
```

Notice a few things about the above code segment. First, we declare this to be the main package on line 1. Then, on line 2, we import the `fmt` package (for formatted I/O).

On line 4, we begin our main function. Notice a few things about this. Firstly, there is no return type. The func is just a keyword declaring that main is a function. But return types in Go are specified *after* the identifier of a function.

On line 5, we call the `Printf()` method of the `fmt` package. This allows us to print to the console. Finally, on line 6, we close the code block with a closing curly brace.

Also, be careful about the opening curly brace, "{". It *must* be on the same line as the declarative header of the main function (and all functions for that matter). Some people prefer programming with the curly brace on a separate line, thusly:

```
func main()
{
```

33

```
    fmt.Printf("Hi there!\n ");
  }
```

However, this will cause a compiler error, such as:

```
hello.go:5:  syntax error near main
```

This may change in the future, but just to be safe, always keep it on the same line as the function header. In fact, keeping everything clean and compact is in line with the Go philosophy of coding.

In case you're curious, the actual reason this causes a compiler error has to do with how and where Go automatically inserts semicolons. So, when you compile the code, the compiler actually reads:

```
func main();
{
  fmt.Printf("Hi there!\n ");
}
```

which is a syntax error.

Go is most certainly concerned with efficiency and tidiness. In fact, let's see what happens if we include another package, but don't use it:

```
1  package main
2  import "fmt"
3  import "os"
4
5  func main(){
6        fmt.Printf("Hi there!\n ");
7  }
```

or, alternatively, with some "shortcut syntax" provided by Go (notice you can put parentheses around the things you're importing, without retyping import. More on this later.):

```
1   package main
2   import
3   (
4     "fmt"
5     "os"
6   )
7
8   func main(){
9   fmt.Printf("Hi there!\n ");
10  }
```

What happens when we try to compile this code?

```
hello.go:5:  imported and not used: os
```

What's this? A compiler error simply because I included a
package I'm not using? You betcha! Go wants to you to
be lean, clean, programming machines. And part of this is
to not include packages you're not using in your code.
They just adds fat to your executables (i.e., they increase
the executable size) and decrease the readability of your
code.

3.1.2 Retrieving Input from the User

Retrieving input from the user is a little bit more
complicated. Some of the syntax may appear a bit strange,
especially if you are brand new to Go. For right now, just
try to follow as best you can, and we'll go over more
details about packages, variable declarations, functions, and
a whole lot more later in the book. Here's the Go code that
we will analyze:

```
1   package main
2
3   import
4   (
5     "fmt"
6     "bufio"
```

```
7    "os"
8  )
9
10  func main(){
11
12      var inputReader *bufio.Reader;   //reader for
input
13      var input string;   //input of type string
14      var err os.Error;
15
16      inputReader = bufio.NewReader(os.Stdin);
17
18      fmt.Printf("Please enter some input: \n");
19
20      input,err = inputReader.ReadString('\n');
21
22      if err == nil{
23          fmt.Printf("The input was : %s\n", input);
24      }
25  }
```

As always, we start at line 1 by naming the package main (there is reasoning behind this, that won't be covered just yet). Then, on lines 3-8, we have our imports. This time, we need a couple more packages than in the input example. We need the os package so we can use Stdin, and we need bufio to perform the retrieval of input from the keyboard.

In the main function, you see on lines 12-14 declarations of variables. Notice that the format of declaring variables in Go is:

```
var identifier  data_type
```

Note that var is a keyword, identifier is the name of the variable, and data_type is the type of data with which we are dealing.

On line 16, we perform the actual creation of the Reader to read input in from the keyboard.

Line 18 prompts the user to enter something (this could ask for a name, a color, favorite animal... pretty much anything).

Line 20 may be very confusing to the reader. Notice there are not one, but *two* variables (`input` of type `string`, and `err` of type `os.Error`) receiving data from the method call `inputReader.ReadString('\n')`. In full, this is:

```
input,err = inputReader.ReadString('\n');
```

Go supports functions and methods returning multiple values. The `ReadString()` method is such a method. We will discuss this in more detail later, but for now, just know that `ReadString()` returns the input string put into the buffer (in this case, from the keyboard, i.e., standard input/Stdin) as its first return value, and returns an error as its second return value. So, two variables are put on the left side of the call to catch both the input from the keyboard, and an error returned by the method. If there are no errors, `ReadString()` returns `nil` for its error return value.

Also, note that the argument to the `ReadString()` method is the newline character ('\n').

Finally, in lines 22-24, we check to ensure there were no errors, and then echo the user's input back to them. For those familiar with `printf()` function from the C programming language, you may have figured out that `%s` is a *specifier* which will match a character string variable (or constant) listed as one of the parameters after the first.

3.2　　　File I/O

In this section, we'll examine a different case of input and output, namely, file input and file output, known collectively as File I/O.

3.2.1   Output to a File

Below, we have some code for sending output to a file

```
1     package main
2     import (
3        "os"
4        "bufio"
5        "fmt"
6     )
7
8     func main(){
9        var outputWriter *bufio.Writer;
      //a writer for output
10       var outputFile *os.File;
      //an output file
11       var outputError os.Error;
      //a variable to catch any error
12       var outputString string;   //the string to print
13
14       // Create file for output
15       outputFile,outputError = os.Open("output.dat",
      os.O_WRONLY|os.O_CREATE,0666);
16
17       if outputError != nil {
18         fmt.Printf("An error occured with file creation\n");
19         return;  //exit the program
20       }
21
22       // Create a new Writer, associated with the
      file we created
23       outputWriter = bufio.NewWriter(outputFile);
24
25       outputString = "hello!\n";
26
27       for i:=0; i<10; i++{
28          outputWriter.WriteString(outputString);
29          outputWriter.Flush();
30       }//end for loop
31    }
```

As always, we have the initial package declaration at the top, followed by import statements:

```
1    package main
2    import(
3      "os"
4      "bufio"
5      "fmt"
6    )
```

Notice that we have the fmt and os packages imported, just like in the standard output example. However, this time, we will utilize the bufio package as well.

In lines 8-12, we have the beginning of our main function, and several variable declarations:

```
8    func main(){
9      var outputWriter *bufio.Writer; //a writer for output
10     var outputFile *os.File;  //an output file
11     var outputError os.Error; //a variable to catch any error
12     var outputString string;  //the string to print
```

Notice the var keyword comes before the name, or *identifier*, of the variable, and then the data type is at the end of the declaration. Also, for some individuals coming from C++, statements like *bufio.Writer may seem a little peculiar. But, it's actually quite natural, when you say the statements out loud. For example, "I'm declaring a *variable* named *outputWriter* that is a *pointer* to a *bufio.Writer*.

It only seems "backwards" if you're accustomed to using a language like C/C++ or Java. It could be argued that the order of the declaration is actually *closer* to natural language (at least to English) than C++, where you may have something like:

```
bufio.Writer* outputWriter; //C++ code
```

In C++, we have the data type first, and then the identifier, and no `var` keyword. If you read it aloud, it becomes, "I'm declaring a *bufio.Writer* pointer called *outputWriter*". This could be refined slightly, but it really is farther from English than the Go syntax is.

Moving on, we create a file to represent the output file we are going to write to:

```
14      // Create file for output
15      outputFile,outputError = os.Open("output.dat",
     os.O_WRONLY|os.O_CREATE,0666);
16
17      if outputError != nil {
18        fmt.Printf("An error occured with file creation\n");
19        return;  //exit the program
20      }
```

Notice in line 15, we are using two of the variables declared earlier, namely, `outputFile` and `outputError` to catch the return values of `os.Open()`. We will explore more on multiple return values later, but for now, just think of `os.Open()` as a machine that produces multiple outputs.

Let's examine the parameters of `os.Open()` carefully:

```
os.Open("output.dat", os.O_WRONLY|
os.O_CREATE,0666);
```

The general signature of the function is as follows:

```
os.Open(filename string, flag int, permissions
int);
```

`Open()` function takes three parameters, in order:

- **The *filename* of type *string*.** This is the name of the file to be used.

- **The *flag*(s) of type *int*.** This lists the flags, indicating what operation(s) we're performing on the file. For example, O_WRONLY for "write only" and O_CREATE for "create", as in our output example. Notice, we can combine them with the *bitwise OR operator*, |.
- **The *permissions* of type *int*.** This parameter includes the access permissions to the file in question. For example, if we are creating a file (as above), and we want the permissions to be full read, write, and execute permissions to users, groups, and others, we would set the permissions to 0777. This corresponds to the chmod command used on Unix to change permissions.

In our particular example, we set the filename of the output file to "output.dat". For the second parameter, we do a bitwise OR of O_WRONLY and O_CREATE to indicate we want to create and/or write to the file, output.dat. Finally, we set the access permissions to 0666, indicating that we want to allow the user, the group, and others to have read and write permissions.

As an experiment, try recompiling the program with the permissions set to different numbers, like 0 (indicating no one has the permission to do anything to the file).

In lines 22-31, we see the remainder of the program:

```
22      // Create a new Writer, associated
        with the file we created
23      outputWriter = bufio.NewWriter(outputFile);
24
25      outputString = "hello!\n";
26
27      for i:=0; i<10; i++{
28          outputWriter.WriteString(outputString);
29      }//end for loop
30      outputWriter.Flush();
31  }
```

On line 23, we create a new `bufio.Writer` object, which is a buffered implementer of `io.Writer`. This allows us to buffer data, before flushing it to an output stream.

We store the string "hello!" followed by a newline character, '\n' into our string, `outputString`. Then, on line 27, we write the header to the `for` loop. Notice that the syntax is slightly different than C++ or Java. There are no parentheses () enclosing the declaration, condition, and incrementing of our counter variable `i`. Also, notice we did not have to declare `i` as in integer explicitly. The `:=` operator takes care of the data typing for us. We will explore this handy little tool later in the book.

Inside the body of the `for` loop, we are essentially appending (buffering) the `outputString` ten times into our `Writer`, `outputWriter`. After the loop has completed, we call `Flush()` to actually send the buffered data to the output file.

To see the results of our application, we have to type:

```
$ 6g file_output.go
$ 6l file_output.6
$ ./6.out
```

Note that should be replaced with whatever you named your program. And unless you used the `-o` option to rename the output executable, `6.out` remains the default executable name.

The output should be as follows:

```
hello!
hello!
```

```
hello!
hello!
hello!
hello!
hello!
hello!
hello!
hello!
```

This is exactly what we expect. There are 10 "hello!" strings printed to the console, each followed by a newline.

3.2.2   *Input from a File*

Below, we have some code for retrieving input from a file, and printing it to the console.

```
1    package main
2    import(
3      "os"
4      "bufio"
5      "fmt"
6    )
7
8    func main(){
9       var inputFile *os.File;   //file for input
10      var inputError os.Error; //variable to catch
    any input file error
11      var readerError os.Error; //variable to catch
    reader errors
12      var inputReader *bufio.Reader; //input reader
13      var inputString string;   //string to catch
    input
14
15      // open the input file
16      inputFile,inputError =
    os.Open("input.dat",os.O_RDONLY,0);
17
18      if inputError !=nil{
19          fmt.Printf("Error opening input file.\n");
20          return;  //exit program
21      }
```

```
22
23    // Create a Reader for input, based on the
   input file
24    inputReader = bufio.NewReader(inputFile);
25
26    for{
27        inputString, readerError =
   inputReader.ReadString('\n');
28
29        if readerError != nil{
30            return; // we've reached EOF (end of
   file) or an error
31        }
32
33        fmt.Printf("The input was : %s",
   inputString);
34    }//end for loop
35 }
```

In this program, lines 1-6 are straightforward. We import the same packages that we required for our file output scenario.

```
8   func main(){
9       var inputFile *os.File;   //file for input
10      var inputError os.Error; //variable to catch
   any input file error
11      var readerError os.Error; //variable to catch
   reader errors
12      var inputReader *bufio.Reader; //input reader
13      var inputString string;   //string to catch
   input
```

Lines 8-13 begin our main function. The variable declarations in lines 9-13 have comments explaining what each does. We need an input file variable, an associated error variable, a reader for the input, and associated error for that, and finally, an input string that will contain the input as it is coming in from the file.

```
15      // open the input file
16      inputFile,inputError =
   os.Open("input.dat",os.O_RDONLY,0);
```

44

```
17
18      if inputError !=nil{
19          fmt.Printf("Error opening input file.\n");
20          return;  //exit program
21      }
```

In line 16, we see that again, we capture the two return values of the Open() function. However, this time, the parameters to Open() are quite different:

```
os.Open("input.dat",os.O_RDONLY,0);
```

In this case, we provide a name for a file that we wish to obtain input from. The second parameter indicates that we are opening this file to read it only, not to do anything else to it. The third parameter is quite useless in this particular scenario, because we are not changing the rights to the file. It isn't our file. We're only opening it to read, so as long as the user set the file permissions appropriately, we can read this file. So, for the third parameter, we just set it to 0.

In lines 18-21 we test to see if there were any errors that occurred while trying to open the input file (input.dat). Errors might occur if the file doesn't exist, or if the file does not indicate sufficient permissions for us to read it. It's good for us to catch any errors, so that we can print out an error message to the user, and then gracefully exit the program.

If we didn't catch errors, and one occurred, the program would almost certainly crash in an ugly mess, horrifying the user and maybe causing mental breakdown, loss of wages, or chronic itchy scalp. In any case, it's good to try to catch errors when we can.

```
23      // Create a Reader for input, based on the
        input file
24      inputReader = bufio.NewReader(inputFile);
```

45

```
25
26    for{
27        inputString, readerError =
      inputReader.ReadString('\n');
28
29        if readerError != nil{
30            break; // we've reached EOF (end of
      file) or an error
31        }
32
33        fmt.Printf("The input was : %s",
      inputString);
34    }//end for loop
35  }
```

After we open the file for reading, we create a
bufio.Reader object on line 24, to be used to read the file.
The parameter to bufio.NewReader is, as was the case in
our writing program, the file we are working with.

In lines 26-34, we see the body of the for loop. Notice in
this case, the for loop has no conditions. This is valid
syntax, and is an infinite loop. There are no while or do-
while loops in Go. The for loop is the only iterative
(looping) structure in the Go language. We will learn about
for loops in more detail later on in this book.

Notice that this loop can be broken out of, if the
readerError is something other than nil. In the vast
majority of cases, the break will be caused by EOF (end of
file) being reached.

And line 35 is the end of the main() function, thus the end
of the program.

If you run the program, assuming you have a file called
input.dat that contains:

chicken

```
cow
donkey
horse
pig
```

You should see the following output to the console:

```
The input was : chicken
The input was : cow
The input was : donkey
The input was : horse
The input was : pig
```

3.2.3   A Short Summary of Permissions

In the code above, some of the talk about "permissions" may have been intimidating if you are not familiar with Unix (or Unix-like systems). On a Unix system, we have a utility called `chmod`, which allows us to change the permissions for particular categories of users.

A typical chmod interaction may look like this:

```
$ chmod 777 myfile.txt
```

In this case the `chmod` command is being called on the `myfile.txt` file, and the permissions are being changed to 777, which basically gives full access to anyone.

Go utilizes the same type of permissions technique with its files, so it is important that we review what these numbers mean.

First, we have to know a little about the three categories of users:

- User
- Group

- Other

The *user* is the owner of the file, which is usually the user who created the file. Sometimes, this can be the individual to whom ownership was assigned (probably with the chown command for reassignment of ownership.)

The *group* includes users who are part of the file's group.

Finally, *other* indicates all other users (users who are not the owner of the file, nor in the file's group).

Now, for each of these, we can assign a number:

User			Group			Other		
Read	Write	Execute	Read	Write	Execute	Read	Write	Execute
4	2	1	4	2	1	4	2	1

This may look a bit confusing at first glance, but we really just add the numbers for the corresponding privilege, within the correct category to get the appropriate number.

For example, if we want the owner of the file to have full permissions (Read, Write, and Execute) we take the three numbers and add them:

$4 + 2 + 1 = 7$

So the first number we will use with chmod is a 7.

Let's say we want the group to have read and write privileges, but no execute privilege. Then, we take the Read (4) and Write (2) and add them:

$4 + 2 + 0 = 6$

So, the access privilege for group is 6.

Finally, for other, let's say we will allow read privilege, but nothing else. So that is:

$4 + 0 + 0 = 4$.

So, in total, our three digit number is:

764

Used with `chmod`, we could type:

```
$ chmod 764 myfile.txt
```

For the `Open()` function in Go, for example, we would use 0764 as the final parameter.

There is one important note to be made about all of this. The *final* permissions of a file depends on a second value, called the *umask*. If you type `umask` at the command line, it should return something like:

0022

Whatever the value of `umask` is, subtract it from the permissions you set with Open(), and that will be the final permissions of the file. For example, if you used 0666 as your permissions parameter to Open(), you get:

$$\begin{array}{r} 0666 \\ - 0022 \\ \hline \mathbf{0644} \end{array}$$

Thus, 0644 is your *actual* permissions for the file that Open() was called upon. The umask could be changed in the .bashrc file if you wished. However, umask is intended primarily to allow the user to limit what programs can do on his/her system in terms of changing permissions.

3.3   Constants and Variables

The Go programming language has syntax that is somewhat different from languages like C++, Java, or C#. We have been introduced to some practical examples of input and output operations in the previous two sections of this chapter. In this section, we will explore how to declare and utilize variables and constants, and we will examine several of the basic data types available in Go.

3.3.1   Identifiers

Valid identifiers in Go begin with a letter (which may be anything identified as a letter in Unicode UTF-8, or an underscore _) followed by zero or more letters or Unicode digits. To clarify in a more concise manner:

```
LETTER = UNICODE_LETTER or "_"

IDENTIFIER = LETTER followed by 0 or more { LETTER or
UNICODE_DIGIT }
```

The following are examples of valid identifiers:

```
q
X56
yoyo
_x23
__65xg
```

θλῖψις

Notice one very important difference with Go. Go uses *Unicode*, not just ASCII letters. So, the identifier θλῖψις in Greek is a valid identifier in Go. Although some issues are still being sorted out in this new, ever changing programming language, it is important to note that the designers of Go have taken a step towards making Go a more internationalized language. This will undoubtedly have far reaching consequences on the future accessibility of programming in non-English speaking nations.

In contrast, the following are not valid identifiers:

```
99sd    //identifiers can't start with numbers!
case    //identifiers can't be Go language reserved words
+2d     //identifiers can't contain operators
```

The underscore by itself, _, is a special identifier known as the *blank identifier* can be used in a declaration or value assignment like any other identifier, but the value is discarded. This may not seem useful right now, but will prove useful in situations such as with functions and methods that return multiple values.

3.3.2   Constants

Constants in Go can only be one of three types:

- Numbers
- Strings
- Booleans

The general form to declare a constant is:

```
const Identifier = value;
```

where `const` is a keyword indicating that the following is a constant, `Identifier` is the name of the constant, and `value` is the value of the constant.

In specific, a constant is declared as follows:

```
const PI = 3.14159;
```

Constants must be able to be evaluated at *compile time*. Calculations are acceptable, as long as they involve values that are able to be evaluated at compile time, and do not require any runtime activities.

For example,

```
const myConst = 2/3;
```

is acceptable, since 2/3 can be evaluated at compile time.

Note that the type specifier is optional.

The following constant declaration will cause a compiler error:

```
const SomeConstant = getMyNumber();
```

Let's assume that `getMyNumber()` is a function that we declared somewhere to simply return the number 5.5, for example.

```
func getMyNumber() float{
    return 5.5;
}
```

Since `getMyNumber()` requires that the program be compiled already, so that the function can be called when the program is executed, we cannot use its return value as the value for `SomeConstant`.

Also, constants are called constant due to the fact that you can't change their value during the execution of the program. The value stays (wait for it...) constant! If you try to reassign a value to a constant, you will get a compiler error, something like:

```
myProgram.go:15:  cannot assign to 7
```

The value you see at the end (7) is the constant's value it was initialized with. So, when the compiler gets to a reassignment statement, such as:

```
myConst = 15;
```

it sees:

```
7 = 15
```

which is obviously an error.

3.3.3   Variables

The general form to declare a variable is:

```
var Identifier DataType = value;
```

where the `var` is a keyword indicating that the following statement will be a variable, `Identifier` is the name of the variable, `DataType` is the type of data that the variable will contain, and `value` is the initial value of the variable.

Variables in Go are similar to constants, except they can be initialized with values computed at runtime.

For example, let's say I wanted to know what the environment variable GOOS is set to. If you recall, during installation, GOOS is the environment variable that indicates the platform (operating system) we installed Go on.

In my case, I can use the following code to determine this particular environment variable's contents:

```
1        package main
2        import(
3            "fmt"
4            "os"
5        )
6
7        func main(){
8            var goos string = os.Getenv("GOOS");
9            fmt.Printf("The operating system is : %s\n",
     goos);
10        }
```

The above code is a complete program, but is very simple. Like other systems languages (such as C/C++), Go allows you to obtain environment variables. The os.Getenv() function takes a single, string parameter and returns a string indicating the contents of the environment variable you specify.

In the case of the computer I'm working on (running Ubuntu), the output of this program would be:

```
The operating system is : linux
```

Also important to note is that, like constants, the data type identifier is optional, as long as there is an initialization expression. One or the other, or both are acceptable.

For example,

```
var t string;
string = "hello";

var t = "hello";
```

are both acceptable. But,

```
var t;
```

is not an acceptable declaration and will cause a compiler error. While Go is forgiving with its unique typing system, it is still *technically* strongly typed. Just declaring `var t;` does not give Go any idea as to what the type of data will be.

3.3.4   Time Savers : Short Declarations and Distributing

So far in this section, we've explored the basics of declaring constants and variables, and initializing their values. However, there are a couple handy tools in our arsenal to make declarations and value assignment statements shorter.

The first of these are *short declarations.* Short declarations allow you to skip having to type the keywords, or even the data type of the variable or constant.

For example,

```
var myInt int = 16;
```

can be shortened to:

```
myInt := 16;
```

In a short declaration, the data type of the identifier myInt is determined by the value it is assigned to. Notice that the := is used for a short declaration, while our old friend the = is used in a traditional declaration.

To shorten even further, it is also acceptable to leave the semicolon (;) off at the end of the declaration. Go automatically inserts a semicolon. My personal preference is to use a semicolon at the end of such statements and expressions.

Another handy technique is *distributing* of a keyword. We've seen this already with our import statements:

```
import(
    "fmt"
    "os"
)
```

The parentheses allow you to distribute the keyword. The above is equivalent to:

```
import "fmt";
import "os";
```

We can use distribution with variables and constants too. It becomes quite cumbersome to have to keep writing the same keyword over and over again, so Go allows us to use this technique to save time when coding, increasing the writability of the language.

```
var(
    numChickens int = 55;
    numHorses int = 6;
    nameCow string;
    nameRooster string;
    numCamels = 12;
)
```

Notice that mixing the data types doesn't matter. All the distribution does is just what its name implies. It distributes the keyword across the identifiers. Notice also that the same rules for declaring all of these separately apply when using distribution. The above is equivalent to:

```
var numChickens int = 55;
var numHorses int = 6;
var nameCow string;
var nameRooster string;
var numCamels = 12;
```

3.4 Some Basic Data Types

Go has many of the data types with which you are probably familiar if you are coming from another language. However, how Go deals with variables and constants of these types may be different than what you're used to. We leave the more complicated and interested data types until later in the book, and focus on some of the more fundamental data types in this section.

3.4.1 Numeric Data Types

Go has a few different *numeric data types* that allow for the storage of numbers. Numbers may include integers or floating point numbers.

The *architecture-dependent* numeric types that Go has predefined are as follows:

```
int
uint
```

```
float
uintptr
```

The `int` type is for storing values that are *integers*,
including both positive and negative values. The `uint`, on
the other hand, stored *unsigned integers*, which means that
values stored for this type can only be positive, but they can
hold larger positive numbers than their `int` counterparts
(because they don't have to leave space for negative values,
they can use it all towards positive values).

The `float` data type is used for numeric values that have
both an integer and fractional data part, such as the value
43.567.

The `uintptr` data type is a special data type that is an
unsigned integer that will be large enough to store a pointer
value.

Note that the sizes of `int`, `uint`, and `float` are dependent
upon the architecture on which they are present. For
example, if you are on a machine with 64 bit architecture,
the int type could be 64 bits, whereas if you are on a 32 bit
machine, the `int` will be 32 bits. The implementation of
the compiler will determine what size `int` will have.
That's why we call these values *architecture-dependent*.

The *architecture-independent* numeric types are:

```
uint8
uint16
uint32
uint64

int8
int16
int32
int64
```

```
float32
float64

byte
```

These types are the size indicated by their names, regardless of the platform on which they reside. For example, the `int8` data type is going to be 8 bits in size, regardless of the platform. The same goes for the other data types.

The `byte` is a familiar alias for `uint8`. This makes sense, since a byte is 8 bits (binary digits) in size.

Also important to note is that Go does not allow implicit type coercion. Let us consider an example program:

```
1       package main
2       import(
3          "fmt"
4       )
5
6       func main(){
7          var my16bitInt int16 = 34;
8          var my32bitInt int32;
9
10         my32bitInt = my16bitInt;
11
12         fmt.Printf("32 bit int is : %d\n", my32bitInt);
13         fmt.Printf("16 bit int is : %d\n", my16bitInt);
14      }
```

This program will generate a compiler error:

```
myFile.go:10:  cannot use my16bitInt (type int16) as
type int32 in assignment
```

Even though both of the variables are integers, Go will not allow us to coerce the value of the 16 bit integer to our 32 bit integer. We have to perform an explicit conversion. To explicitly convert one type to another, you can use the name of the type you are converting *to* with function call syntax. For example, to correct the above program, we would change line 10 from:

```
10        my32bitInt = my16bitInt;
```

to

```
10        my32bitInt = int32(my16bitInt);
```

Now, the program will compile, link, and execute correctly.

Go will also not allow implicit type coercion between different numeric types like int to float, and float to int. You must also explicitly convert these types as well.

And, note that even with conversion, if you assign a float value to an integer variable, the fractional part of the float value will be *truncated* (that is, removed, or lost). For example, if your float variable contains 3.14159, and you try to assign it to an integer variable, with conversion, the integer will only contain 3. You will lose the 0.14159 part of the float value.

3.4.2 Character Data Type

Like most high level languages, Go has a character data type, `char`, which is used to store single characters. One interesting thing about Go, however, is that character data in Go is stored in UTF-8 (Unicode), not ASCII. So, you can store characters from other character or symbol systems.

Characters are essentially numbers that indicate a special encoding. In the case of Go, we can use the traditional ASCII code, such as:

```
var myChar byte = 'c';
```

Notice that we use the data type byte to store a simple ASCII character. Alternatively, we can use the ASCII encoding with the escape character at the beginning, to achieve the same value:

```
var myChar byte = '\x63';
```

If you are not familiar with encoding, don't be frightened. You can fairly easily find ASCII and Unicode tables online. The ASCII hexadecimal (base 16) value for the character 'c' is 63. Don't be fooled. This isn't the same as the decimal (base 10) number *sixty three*. It is actual 99 in decimal. And, as you may suspect, you can write:

```
var myChar byte = 99;
```

Now, to print out the value, you can use the following:

```
fmt.Printf("The character is %c\n", myChar);
```

Note the %c to indicate that the value is to be interpreted as character data.

The \x in the earlier value of \x63 indicates that the number following it is to be interpreted as hexadecimal.

Now, we have mentioned that Go supports Unicode. In order to use Unicode, you preface the value with the \ escape character, and the a u. The number that follows is hexadecimal, and indicates a UTF-8 encoded character.

For example, to store the Greek letter Beta (β), we use the following encoding:

```
var myBeta int = '\u03B2';
```

This is because the Unicode encoding for the Greek letter Beta is 03B2. Note that this time, instead of a `byte`, we needed to use an `int`. This is because a `byte` (8-bits) is too small to hold the Unicode UTF-8 encoding of a character.

If the console you are using is capable of rendering UTF-8 encoded characters, you can declare and print out any of the UTF-8 encoded characters. This gives you the ability to print characters from a wide array of language character sets, including Chinese, Japanese, Arabic, Bengalese, Hindi, Greek, and Armenian, just to name a few.

3.4.3   *Boolean Data Type*

The *Boolean* data type is pretty straightforward. Boolean data are used to represent truth values, and can only contain one of two values, `true` or `false`. An example of Boolean data in use will follow:

```
1      package main
2      import(
3        "fmt"
4      )
5
6      func main(){
7        var myBool bool;
8        myBool = false;
9
10       if myBool==false{
11         fmt.Printf("the value is false\n");
12       }else{
13         fmt.Printf("the value is true\n");
14       }
```

```
15      }
```

In this program, we create a Boolean variable on line 7 and set its value to `false` on line 8. Then, to see an example (albeit trivial) of how a Boolean variable may be used, we see an if-else statement on lines 10-14.

We will explore if-else statements in more detail later, but for now, you just need to know that if-else statements are one of the control structures to allow a computer program to make decisions.

3.5   The `string` Data Type

I've devoted an entire section to the string data type, because there is a lot of useful information about strings that I thought deserved its own section. This is not to say that there aren't many other interesting things we could do with Booleans or integers (which we will see more of later), but strings in Go are quite interesting.

So what is a string, exactly? In Go, the *string* data type represents a *concatenated*, or connected, sequence of characters. Unlike languages like C++, strings in Go are *immutable*, which means that once the string is created, you cannot modify its contents. For example, in C++, you can modify individual characters within the string. Go does not allow this.

Also, in Go, strings are not NULL-terminated, but rather length delimited. In other words, there is no \0, at the end of the character string.

In Go, there are two forms of strings:

- Interpreted Strings

- Raw Strings

Interpreted strings are nearly identical to the strings that are familiar to readers who may be familiar with other languages. An interpreted string is surrounded by double quotes (" "), and escape sequences are interpreted.

Raw strings, are strings that are not interpreted. The are surrounded by the back quotes (` `, also known as *grave accent*). On a standard keyboard, the grave accent is located on the same key as the tilde (~), to the left of the number keys.

The following is an example of the differences between interpreted and raw strings:

```
1     package main
2     import(
3       "fmt"
4     )
5
6     func main(){
7         var myRawString string;
8         var myInterString string;
9
10        myRawString = `This is a raw string  \n`;
11        myInterString = "This is an interpreted string \n";
12
13        fmt.Printf("Here is the string: %s\n",
          myRawString);
14        fmt.Printf("Here is the other string: %s\n",
          myInterString);
15
16    }
```

The output of the above program is:

```
johnbaugh@ubuntu:~/Desktop/go_programming/strings$ ./6.out
Here is the string: This is a raw string  \n
Here is the other string: This is an interpreted string

johnbaugh@ubuntu:~/Desktop/go_programming/strings$
```

Notice that in the first string (the raw string), the \n is printed as if it were simply a backslash followed by the character 'n'. In the interpreted string, the \n is interpreted as the newline character, which is why there is a blank line present in the output of the program.

While immutable, strings are accessible via standard indexing methods. For example, if I wanted to access the first character in a particular string, I can use the following code segment:

```
var someString string = "My name is John";
fmt.Printf("The first character is %c\n", someString[0]);
```

The character at `someString[0]` is 'M'. Index 0 is the first character in the string. To know the index of the last character in any particular string is to use the universally available `len()` function. Since the first character of the string is at 0, then the last character is at the length of the string minus 1. So, to print out the last character of the string we described above, we use the following code:

```
fmt.Printf("The first character is %c\n",
someString[len(someString)-1]);
```

Make sure that you put the -1 after the length function is called, or there will be a runtime error.

3.5.1 The strings Package

In this subsection, we'll explore some of the functionality of a package that Go provides for simple string manipulation, the `strings` package. I will not cover all of the functions available in this package, but will try to give you some idea about what you can do with strings in Go using the functionality available in this package.

Prefixes and Suffixes

To determine if a particular string begins or ends with a particular character or substring, Go provides us with a couple very handy functions in the `strings` package.

```
strings.HasPrefix(str string, prefix string) bool;

strings.HasSuffix(str string, suffix string) bool;
```

As you may recall from your studies in English, a *prefix* is the beginning of a word (or for our purposes, the beginning of a string), and a *suffix* is the end of a word (or string).

Each of the functions above returns a Boolean value (either `true` or `false`), and they both take a string to search within as their first parameter (the formal parameter `str` in the above function prototypes).

For both of these functions, the second parameter indicates a substring you are searching for. The function `HasPrefix` will return `true` if the second parameter `prefix` is the substring that `str` *begins* with, and `false` otherwise. Similarly, the `HasSuffix` function will return `true` if the second parameter `suffix` is the substring that `str` ends with, and `false` otherwise.

Here is an example of `HasPrefix` and `HasSuffix` in action:

```
1    package main
2    import(
3      "fmt"
4      "strings"
5    )
6
7    func main(){
8        var myString string = "This is a string";
```

```
9
10      fmt.Printf("T/F? Does the string \"%s\" have prefix
        %s?: ", myString,"Th");
11      fmt.Printf("%v\n", strings.HasPrefix(myString,
        "Th"));
12
13      fmt.Printf("T/F? Does the string \"%s\" have prefix
        %s?: ", myString, "X");
14      fmt.Printf("%v\n", strings.HasPrefix(myString,
        "X"));
15
16      fmt.Printf("T/F? Does the string \"%s\" have suffix
        %s?: ", myString, "ing");
17      fmt.Printf("%v\n", strings.HasSuffix(myString,
        "ing"));
18
19      fmt.Printf("T/F? Does the string \"%s\" have suffix
        %s?: ", myString, "cow");
20      fmt.Printf("%v\n", strings.HasSuffix(myString,
        "cow"));
21
22   }
```

The output of the above program is as follows:

```
johnbaugh@ubuntu:~/Desktop/go_programming/presuf$ ./6.out
T/F? Does the string "This is a string" have prefix Th?:
true
T/F? Does the string "This is a string" have prefix X?:
false
T/F? Does the string "This is a string" have suffix ing?:
true
T/F? Does the string "This is a string" have suffix cow?:
false
```

Let's briefly examine the program code above. The fmt
package is imported, along with the package we're learning
about, the strings package on lines 3 and 4.

On line 8, we declare and initialize the string that we are
going to work with.

In lines 10, 13, 16, and 19, we echo the string and the
prefix or suffix we are going to test for. Notice the usage
of \"%s\" to ensure that quotes are printed in the actual

output. The usage of the backslash in front of the quotation mark ensures that the quotation mark is *escaped*, or, ignored as a part of the languages syntax. If you do not escape quotations or other components of the Go language, the compiler will flag them as syntax errors.

In line 11, we test for the prefix "Th", using the functions `HasPrefix()`. Since our string, `myString`, has the prefix "Th", this function returns `true`. In line 14, we test for a prefix of "X", which causes HasPrefix() to return false.

Similarly, we can test for suffixes. In lines 17, and 20 we test for "ing" and "cow" respectively as suffixes. Since "ing" is a suffix of our sentence, `HasSuffix()` returns `true`. However, for the test of "cow", `HasSuffix()` returns `false`.

The output is what we expect. For the prefix "Th", and later, the suffix "ing", the output is `true`. But, for the prefix "X", and the suffix "cow", the output is `false`, since these are not a prefix and suffix of `myString`, respectively.

Counting Occurrences of a Substring

Sometimes, it may be useful to know how many occurrences of a particular substring are in a string. The following function is for this very purpose:

```
strings.Count(str string, sub string) int;
```

The exact definition says that the function `strings.Count()` returns the "number of non-overlapping instances of sub in str".

What exactly does this mean? Well, let's consider some code:

```
1    package main
2    import(
3      "fmt"
4      "strings"
5    )
6
7    func main(){
8        var myString string = "Hello how is it going,
     Harold?";
9        var manyA string = "aaaaaaaaaa";
10
11       fmt.Printf("Number of H's in %s is :", myString);
12       fmt.Printf("%d\n", strings.Count(myString,"H"));
13
14       fmt.Printf("Number of double a's in %s is : ",
     manyA);
15       fmt.Printf("%d\n", strings.Count(manyA,"aa"));
16   }
```

And the output of the above program is:

```
johnbaugh@ubuntu:~/Desktop/go_programming/countsubst$ ./6.o
ut
Number of H's in Hello how is it going, Harold? is :2
Number of double a's in aaaaaaaaaa is : 5
```

Notice in the code (and the corresponding output) that in lines 11-12, we test the string myString for the single, one character long substring, "H". This returns a count of 2, because there are 2 of the capital letter "H" in our string, myString (one in "Hello", and one in "Harold").

To demonstrate what is meant by "non-overlapping instances...", consider the string, manyA, which has 10 of the lower case letter "a" in a row. We then test for the number of occurrences of double a's. The resulting count is 5. Why 5? Let's compare overlapping instances with non-overlapping:

Non-overlapping instance of "aa":

Count	
1	**aa**aaaaaaaa
2	aa**aa**aaaaaa
3	aaaa**aa**aaaa
4	aaaaaa**aa**aa
5	aaaaaaaa**aa**

As you can see, with non-overlapping instances of "aa", you move on to the "a" following the last "a" in the double a ("aa") that you just counted.

If the Count() function considered overlapping instances, it would count 9 such instances:

Count	
1	**aa**aaaaaaaa
2	a**aa**aaaaaaa
3	aa**aa**aaaaaa
4	aaa**aa**aaaaa
5	aaaa**aa**aaaa
6	aaaaa**aa**aaa
7	aaaaaa**aa**aa
8	aaaaaaa**aa**a
9	aaaaaaaa**aa**

In the case of *overlapping* instances, we see that we use the last "a" of the double a we just counted as the first "a" of the next double a we are about to count.

So, just remember that strings.Count() *does not* count overlapping instances.

Index and LastIndex

Often, we want to know at what position a particular character or substring occurs in a string. Go provides two helpful functions that accomplish this task:

```
strings.Index(str string, sub string) int;

strings.LastIndex(str string, sub string) int;
```

Both of these functions return -1 if they cannot find the substring in question.

If the substring being searched for does exist in the string str, the Index() function will return the index of the first instance of sub in str, while LastIndex(), not surprisingly, returns the last index of sub in str.

As an example, consider the following code:

```
1    package main
2    import(
3      "fmt"
4      "strings"
5    )
6
7    func main(){
8      var myString string;
9      myString = "Hi, I'm John. Hi.";
10
11     fmt.Printf("The position of \"John\" is: ");
12     fmt.Printf("%d\n", strings.Index(myString, "John"));
13
14     fmt.Printf("The position of the last instance
     of \"Hi\" is: ");
15     fmt.Printf("%d\n", strings.LastIndex(myString,
     "Hi"));
16
17     fmt.Printf("the position of \"Burger\" is: ");
18     fmt.Printf("%d\n", strings.Index(myString,
     "Burger"));
19
```

```
20  }
```

And the output from the above code is as follows:

```
johnbaugh@ubuntu:~/Desktop/go_programming/index$ ./6.out
The position of "John" is: 8
The position of the last instance of "Hi" is: 14
the position of "Burger" is: -1
```

The code and its corresponding output shows us three different scenarios involving the finding of an index of a particular substring. The first, on lines 11-12, uses the Index() function to search for the string "John". This returns 8, because the 'J' in "John" occurs at position 8. Secondly, we use LastIndex() to search for the substring "Hi". Notice that "Hi" occurs twice in our string, myString.

LastIndex() returns the *last* occurrence of the substring "Hi", which is why the function did not return a 0 (for the index of the 'H' in the first "Hi"), but rather it returned 14, because 14 is the index of the 'H' in the last "Hi" in the string.

Finally, we used Index() to search for a string that does not exist as a substring inside of myString. Since "Burger" is not inside myString, the function returns -1. This is a clever return value that many programming languages use to indicate that a value was not found. Since all indices (the plural of *index*) have non-negative values (e.g. 0, 1, 2, 3, ...) we know that any negative value would never be used as an actual index. So, the programmers of Go chose -1 to indicate the substring was not found.

72

Repeat

If we have a string that we want to copy several times and place in a new string, we have a quick and easy way to do this, with the following function:

```
strings.Repeat(str string, count int) string;
```

The function prototype for `Repeat()` has two parameters. The first, `str` of type `string` indicates which string we wish to copy. The second, `count` of type `int`, indicates how many times we want to repeat the string. And, the return type, indicated at the end of the prototype is `string`.

The following code demonstrates the usage of the `Repeat()` function:

```
1    package main
2    import(
3      "fmt"
4      "strings"
5    )
6
7    func main(){
8      var origString string = "Hi there ";
9      var newString string;
10
11     newString = strings.Repeat(origString, 3);
12     fmt.Printf("New, repeated string is: %s\n",
       newString);
13   }
```

And the output is:

```
johnbaugh@ubuntu:~/Desktop/go_programming/repeat$ ./6.out
New, repeated string is: Hi there Hi there Hi there
```

In the above code, notice that I included a space at the end of the original string, `origString` on line 8. This is so when I create the value to place in `newString`, it will be more readable when we print it.

The actual function call occurs on line 11, and is fairly straightforward. We tell the `Repeat()` function that we want it to return a new string that uses our `origString`, and repeats it 3 times.

ToUpper and ToLower

Two very common tasks in programming involve change the case of strings. One obvious example would be when a user signs up for a particular website. The user creates a login name and password, and various other information. Consider what a nightmare it would be (and is, on some websites) if the user's login name was case sensitive. Often, web developers will perform a `tolower()` of whatever language they are working with on the initial registration, and on subsequent logins, so that no matter what case the user uses, they can still log into their account.

Go offers both `ToUpper()` and `ToLower()` functions.

Their prototypes are essentially identical:

```
strings.ToUpper(str string) string;

strings.ToLower(str string) string;
```

The `ToUpper()` function returns a new string in which all characters in the parameter `str` are changed to upper case.

The `ToLower()` function, on the other hand, returns a string in which all characters in the parameter `str` are changed to lower case.

If a particular character is already in the appropriate case, or does not have a corresponding upper or lower case character (such as numbers or special symbols), then the character is left alone.

Consider the following code:

```
1    package main
2    import(
3      "fmt"
4      "strings"
5    )
6
7    func main(){
8        var origString string = "Hey, how are you, George?";
9        var lowerString string;
10       var upperString string;
11
12       lowerString = strings.ToLower(origString);
13       upperString = strings.ToUpper(origString);
14
15       fmt.Printf("Original string : %s\n", origString);
16       fmt.Printf("Lowercase string : %s\n", lowerString);
17       fmt.Printf("Uppercase string : %s\n", upperString);
18   }
```

And the output is:

```
johnbaugh@ubuntu:~/Desktop/go_programming/upper_lower$ ./6.
out
Original string : Hey, how are you, George?
Lowercase string : hey, how are you, george?
Uppercase string : HEY, HOW ARE YOU, GEORGE?
```

In this program, we create our original string on line 8, and assign it the value "Hey, how are you, George?". Then, we declare two strings, lowerString and upperString on lines 9 and 10. These are then used on lines 12 and 13 to capture the values returned by ToLower() and ToUpper(), respectively, when applied to origString.

Finally, on lines 15-17, we print the various strings that we've created.

Pay close attention to the output. Notice that for the lowercase string, the 'H' from "Hey" and the 'G' from "George" in the original string are changed to lowercase, but that all the other characters (that are already lowercase) are not modified.

Similarly, for the uppercase string, all of the lowercase characters are changed to uppercase, and those that are already uppercase do not change.

3.5.2 *The strconv Package*

Another package that is useful when dealing with strings is the strconv package. This package offers several functions to convert to and from the string data type. I will give a few examples, but will not go into incredible detail about this package. The usage of the functions is mostly straightforward, and many are very similar. The verbose documentation is available on the official Go website (*http://www.golang.org*).

However, to get an idea of how to use a couple the useful functions and externally available variables that strconv has to offer, consider the following code:

```
1    package main
2    import(
3      "fmt"
4      "os"
5      "strconv"
6    )
7
8    func main(){
9        var origString string = "365";
10       var theInt int;
11       var myNewString string;
12       var err os.Error;
13
```

76

```
14      fmt.Printf("The size of floats is : %d\n",
    strconv.FloatSize);
15      fmt.Printf("The size of ints is: %d\n",
    strconv.IntSize);
16
17      theInt, err = strconv.Atoi(origString);
18
19      if err == nil{
20        fmt.Printf("the integer is : %d\n", theInt);
21      }
22
23      theInt = theInt + 5;   //use as an integer
24
25      myNewString = strconv.Itoa(theInt);
26
27      fmt.Printf("The new string is: %s\n", myNewString);
28
29  }
```

And the output is as follows:

```
johnbaugh@ubuntu:~/Desktop/go_programming/stringconversion$
./6.out
The size of floats is : 32
The size of ints is: 32
the integer is : 365
The new string is: 370
```

In this code, on lines 14 and 15, strconv.FloatSize and
strconv.IntSize are printed out. These give you the size
of the floats and ints, respectively.

Further down, we use strconv.Atoi() function, which
stands for "ASCII to Integer", allowing us to convert a
well-formed string into an integer. In our example, we use
the origString, "365". It is then converted, on line 17, to
the integer value 365:

```
theInt, err = strconv.Atoi(origString);
```

Notice there are two values being captured: the actual
integer and any possible error return if the conversion was

unsuccessful, which may occur, if for instance the string did not represent an integer.

While this may not seem like much of a change, I perform arithmetic on line 17, by adding 5 to our integer that we obtained via the `Atoi()` function. The new value of `theInt` is 370.

Then, on line 25 `theInt` is converted back to a `string`:

```
myNewString = strconv.Itoa(theInt);
```

Now, `myNewString` contains a string representing `theInt`. Recall that `theInt` is now 370, so the string that is returned by `Itoa()` is "370".

3.6   Keywords and Operators

In this section, I'll show you the available keywords and operators that Go has to offer. I will not go into incredible detail in this section, as this section is only here to make you aware of the available keywords, operators, delimiters and other special tokens available in Go. Much of this will be straightforward, and if you are familiar with another high level programming language, much of this will seem familiar. However, Go does have some keywords (also called *reserved words*) that are unique to the language.

3.6.1   Keywords

The following are the keywords of the Go language:

break	default	func	interface	select
case	defer	go	map	struct

chan	else	goto	package	switch
const	fallthrough	if	range	type
continue	for	import	return	var

We have seen a few of these keywords thus far, and some of these may look familiar to people who program in other programming languages. Note that identifiers cannot have the same name as any of the keywords.

The `func` keyword designates the beginning of a function definition. The `var` keyword designates the beginning of a variable. The `const` keyword, similarly, denotes the beginning of a constant definition.

We have briefly utilized, but not thoroughly explained (yet) several other keywords, such as `if`, `else`, and `for`. We will more thoroughly explore these structures later in this book.

There are also several very unique keywords that may look alien to newcomers to the Go programming language. These include keywords like `chan` and `go`. We will also explore these later after we have a stronger foundation in the fundamentals of the language, as they make up some of the more powerful features of Go.

3.6.2   Operators

In the Go language, the following are available operators, delimiters, and other special tokens:

+	&	+=	&=	&&	==	!=	(	)
-	|	-=	|=	||	<	<=	[	]
*	^	*=	^=	<-	>	>=	{	}
/	<<	/=	<<=	++	=	:=	,	;
%	>>	%=	>>=	--	!	...	.	:

79

&^	&^=							

Many of the operators listed are probably very familiar. The `+`, `-`, `*`, `/`, `==`, `++`, `--` and others are quite straightforward. The delimiters such as parentheses `( )`, brackets `[ ]`, and braces, `{ }` should also look familiar.

Others, such as `<-`, `:=`, `&^` may look very foreign to you. We will look into many of the available operators later in this book.

3.7   Summary

In this chapter, we have explored some of the fundamental techniques and building blocks used in Go. We have explored how to retrieve input from the keyboard, as well as from an input file. Also, we learned how to produce output, both to the console, and to an output file.
We explored many of the fundamental data types available with Go. We extensively explored `strings`, and some of the packages used to work with `string` data.

Finally, we briefly introduced the keywords and operators available in Go.

Chapter 4

Control Structures and Functions

Like most high level languages, Go has control structures to allow programs to perform tasks such as making decisions (*conditional structures*) and repeating tasks (*iterative* or *looping structures*). It is rare when any significant program simply performs a linear sequence of tasks. More often than not, programs are full of decisions and repetitive tasks.

Also, in this chapter, we will explore functional decomposition in Go. With functions, we can take a frequently used sequence of instructions and give them a name, to be used over and over again without having to rewrite the same code over and over.

4.1   Conditional Structures

With conditional structures, we can control the execution of a program, allowing the program to make decisions based on the current program state, values of variables, and values of constants. Go offers two conditions structures: the `if` structure and the `switch` structure.

4.1.1   Basics of Logic

This subsection serves as a review of logic so that we can more effectively explore the conditional structures of Go.

Equality

`==` is the equality operator that takes two operands. It is read as "is equal to". Notice there are two equal signs, one followed by the other.

If we have a variable set to the value 6:

```
var someVar int = 6;
```

Give this,

       `someVar == 2` is a false statement
       `someVar == 6` is a true statement

AND operator

The AND operator is a logical binary operator, denoted by `&&`. Logical AND takes two operands, and the entire statement is true *only if* both operands are true.

Given `T` representing a value that is true, and `F` representing a value that is false:

`T && T` is true
`T && F` is false
`F && T` is false
`F && F` is false

OR operator

The OR operator is a logical binary operator, denoted by
||. Logical OR takes two operands, and the entire
statement is true if *any* of the operands are true.

Given T representing a value that is true, and F representing
a value that is false:

T || T is true
T || F is true
F || T is true
F || F is false

The only situation in which a statement involving OR is
false is if both operands are false. Otherwise, as long as at
least one of the operands is true, the statement is true.

NOT operator

The NOT operator is a logical unary operator, denoted by
!. Logical NOT takes one operand, and makes the truth
value of its operand the opposite of what it is:

```
!T   is false
!F   is true
```

4.1.2   The if Structure

For those familiar with other high level languages, the if
structure will look very familiar. The syntax, however,
maybe slightly different than what you may be accustom to.

The if structure takes the basic form:

```
if condition{
```

83

```
        //do something
}
```

Also, there is an optional `else` or `else if` as part of the `if` statement.

```
if condition{
        //do something
} else if condition{
        //do something else
} else{
        //default
}
```

Notice very carefully that with Go, the `else if` and `else` statements *must* be on the same line as the closing curly brace of the previous part of the structure. Also, just like functions (such as the main function that we are so familiar with), the opening curly brace must be on the same line as the `if` statement header and condition.

The following is a syntax error:

```
if condition
{
        //do something
}
```

Also, notice that with proper syntax, there are no parentheses surrounding the condition.

Another form of the `if` statement involves initialization in the header, as follows:

```
if initialization_statement; condition{
        //do something
}
```

The initialization statement must be separated from the condition with a semicolon.

Up until now, we've seen the general forms that `if` statements can take. One of the best ways to understand concepts is in the contexts they will be used. So, as an example of how to use `if`-statements, consider the following:

```
1    package main
2    import(
3      "fmt"
4    )
5
6    func main(){
7        var firstInt int = 10;
8        var condInt int;
9
10       if firstInt <= 0{
11          fmt.Printf("First int is less than or equal to
     0\n");
12        }else if firstInt >0 && firstInt < 5{
13          fmt.Printf("First int is between 0 and 5\n");
14        }else{
15          fmt.Printf("First int is 5 or greater\n");
16        }
17
18
19       if condInt = 5; condInt > 10{
20          fmt.Printf("condInt is greater than 10\n");
21        }else{
22          fmt.Printf("condInt is not greater than 10\n");
23        }
24   }
```

The output of the above code is as follows:

```
johnbaugh@ubuntu:~/Desktop/go_programming/if_else$ ./6.out
First int is 5 or greater
condInt is not greater than 10
```

This is example contains variables that were initialized with literal values in the code itself, and is fairly trivial for the sake of brevity. It is more common that values are input from the user or from a file, and stored in the variables.

In the above example, we show the two different element forms available for if statements. On line 7 we declare and initialize the variable `firstInt`. On line 8 we declare the variable `condInt`.

On lines 10-16, the `firstInt` variable is tested, and the appropriate branch is taken depending on its value. Since the value 10 is stored into `firstInt` statically, we know which branch the program will take (namely, the final `else` branch).

Notice the usage of <= on line 10. This is the less than or equal to sign. Thus, if `firstInt` was a negative number or 0, then the first branch would be taken.

Since this is not the case, the second branch condition is tested: `firstInt >0 && firstInt < 5`. The && (logical AND) indicates that both of its operands must be true in order for the entire statement to be true. In this case, the branch will be followed if the integer is strictly between 0 and 5. Again, this is not the case.

An `else` without any if attached serves as a sort of catch-all. In other words, if all of the above statements that were evaluated are false, the `else` branch will be followed.

On lines 19-23, we see a different form of the `if` statement. In this case, we perform a value assignment to the variable on line 19, as part of the `if` statement's header. After initializing `condInt`, we test its value to determine if it is greater than 10. Like with our first example, we also have an `else` statement that acts as a catch all.

As a final note on `if` statements, you *could* use parentheses around the condition, but it is not typical in Go programming. It is, however, useful in situations where

you may wish (or need) to group logical statements, such as
`if !(var1 == var2)`.

4.1.3   The `switch` *Structure*

Another conditional structure available in Go is the
`switch` structure. These `switch` structures are somewhat
similar to what you may have used in C/C++, but do not
require that you use constants or `int`s as your conditional
values.

Also, you can use multiple `case`s, separating them by
commas.

One major difference between Go and C/C++ `switch`
structures is the `case`s do *not* have automatic fall-through.
In C/C++ and similar languages, you must use a `break;`
statement to ensure that after one `case` is determined to be
true, the switch statement is completed and other `case`s
(such as `default`) are not executed. With Go, as soon as a
`case` is determined to be true, the `switch` is complete, and
program control is returned back to the outer structure
(such as the `main` function).

You can cause automatic fall-through (thus behaving
similarly to how C/C++ `switch` structures behave without
`break` statements) using the Go keyword `fallthrough`.

Let's consider a typical example of how the `switch`
structure is used:

```
1    package main
2    import(
3      "fmt"
4    )
5
6    func main(){
```

```
7      var someNum int = 5;
8
9      switch someNum{
10       case 7: fmt.Printf("It's equal to 7\n");
11       case 5: fmt.Printf("It's equal to 5\n");
12       default: fmt.Printf("It's not 5 or 7\n");
13     }//end switch
14   }
```

And here is the output from the above program:

```
johnbaugh@ubuntu:~/Desktop/go_programming/switch1$ ./6.out
It's equal to 5
```

This is a trivial example, in that we know exactly what the value of `someNum` is, since we initialized its value to 5 and did not change it before entering the conditional evaluation in the `switch` structure header. But, as has been typical, I am simply introducing the concept and example. We can use it and build upon our knowledge in practice, and in examples later in the book.

In this example, we write our `switch` keyword, followed by the variable (in this case) to be evaluated. Then, with each of the `case` statements, our variable `someNum` is compared to the value indicated. For example, on line 10:

```
10       case 7: fmt.Printf("It's equal to 7\n");
```

If `someNum` is equal to 7, we print the string "It's equal to 7", followed by a newline, to the console.

In our situation, the test on line 10 evaluates to `false`, since `someNum` is not equal to 7. Thus, it tries the next `case` statement on line 11. Since this evaluates to `true`, since `someNum` is equal to 5, the output is printed, and the `switch` structure is exited. In C/C++, we would have needed to put a `break;` statement. But, as we discussed earlier, this is not what happens with Go.

Now, let's consider an example that uses strings:

```
1     package main
2     import(
3       "fmt"
4       "os"
5       "bufio"
6     )
7
8     func main(){
9         var inputReader *bufio.Reader;
10        var input string;
11        var err os.Error;
12        inputReader = bufio.NewReader(os.Stdin);
13
14        fmt.Printf("Please enter your name:\n");
15        input,err = inputReader.ReadString('\n');
16
17        if(err != nil){
18            fmt.Printf("There were errors reading.  Exiting
      program\n");
19            return;
20        }
21
22        switch input{
23          case "John\n" :
24            fmt.Printf("Welcome, John!\n");
25          case "Silas\n" :
26            fmt.Printf("Welcome, Silas!\n");
27          default:
28            fmt.Printf("You are not welcome here!  Be
      gone!\n");
29        }//end switch
30    }
```

And here is the interaction output from different test cases:

```
johnbaugh@ubuntu:~/Desktop/go_programming/string_switch$ ./
6.out
Please enter your name:
George
You are not welcome here!  Be gone!
johnbaugh@ubuntu:~/Desktop/go_programming/string_switch$ ./
6.out
Please enter your name:
John
Welcome, John!
johnbaugh@ubuntu:~/Desktop/go_programming/string_switch$ ./
6.out
Please enter your name:
```

89

```
Silas
Welcome, Silas!
```

In this example, we have declared the variables required to interact with the user through the command line. In lines 22-29, we see the `case` statements in our `switch` structure. Since the `ReadString()` function returns the string read from the input stream (`os.Stdin` in our case) up to and *including* the delimiter, we must take the delimiter into consideration when switching on the string variable `input`. This is why we have the newline character at the end of the strings we're comparing `input` against.

This program could be seen as an (albeit oversimplified and insecure) authentication system. There are only two usernames that are considered authenticated users, namely "John" and "Silas". Otherwise, (`default`) the user is not authenticated, and the program tells them, in no uncertain terms, that they are not welcome.

We could have written a program similar to the above program using the `fallthrough` keyword, by rewriting the `switch` structure as follows:

```
switch input{
case "John\n" :
  fallthrough;
case "Silas\n" :
  fmt.Printf("Welcome, %s", input);
default:
  fmt.Printf("You are not welcome here!  Be gone!\n");
}//end switch
```

In this case, regardless of whether the user is John or Silas, we simply want to welcome them. This is thanks to the `fallthrough` keyword, which causes the `case` for "John\n" to perform the action(s) in the next `case` statement. Thus, we can use the `%s` modifier to dynamically insert the user's input into the output string (either "John" or "Silas").

And, another way to consider multiple `case` statements is to separate the values by commas. Thus, the above switch statement can be rewritten as:

```
switch input{
case "John\n","Silas\n" :
   fmt.Printf("Welcome, %s", input);
default:
   fmt.Printf("You are not welcome here!  Be gone!\n");
}//end switch
```

Another form of the `switch` statement can be used to very accurately simulate `if-else` chains. In this form, there is no expression after the `switch` keyword, so the `cases` switch on `true`. This means that if the logical expression following the `case` statement is `true`, the body of the `case` will be executed.
The following code is an example of this type of expressionless `switch` statement:

```
1    package main
2    import(
3       "fmt"
4    )
5
6    func main(){
7       var someNumber int = 5;
8
9       switch{
10        case someNumber < 0:
11            fmt.Printf("Some number is negative\n");
12        case someNumber > 0 && someNumber < 10:
13            fmt.Printf("Some number is between 0 and
     10\n");
14        default:
15            fmt.Printf("Some number is 10 or greater\n");
16     }
17   }
```

And the output of the above code is:

```
johnbaugh@ubuntu:~/Desktop/go_programming/noexp_switch$ ./6
.out
Some number is between 0 and 10
```

In the above code, we now see that the `switch` structure has no expression, and to the astute reader, looks very similar to an `if-else` structure. Often, `switch` statements are helpful, especially with a large number of comparisons. The syntax is often more readable, and even more writable than `if-else` statements.

4.2   Iteration

It is common for a program to repeat a particular task multiple times. In this section, we will explore how to perform iteration with the Go programming language. Go has only one iterative construct, the `for` loop. This may seem peculiar to readers coming from other languages, like C/C++ or Java, which have iterative constructs like `while` loops and `do-while` loops.

In these programming languages, the `for` loop is used most typically (and some would argue, most correctly) in a manner known as *count-controlled iteration*, that is, when a particular number of iterations is required, and known before the loop is entered. Iterative constructs such as `while` and `do-while` in these languages serve as *event-controlled* loops. This means that they are ideally suited for when a particular event must occur in order to exit the loop. However, the programmer doesn't *have to* use them in the prescribed manner.

In Go, the `for` loop allows for a little more flexibility, and can be easily used for both event and count controlled scenarios.

The following code will be an example of the fairly typical usage of the `for` loop:

```
1    package main
2    import(
3      "fmt"
4    )
5
6    func main(){
7
8        for i:=0; i < 5; i++{
9           fmt.Printf("I'm in the %d iteration\n", i);
10       }//end for loop
11   }
```

This is a very typical and simple example of using the `for` loop in the manner that is most familiar to readers coming from many other high level languages. In this form, the `for` loop has an *initialization*, a *conditional check*, and a *modification* of the variable, i. Notice that there are no parentheses surrounding the header of the `for` loop.

Also notice that I use the short declaration format for the counter variable. This could be rewritten with the counter variable declared outside and before the `for` loop, as follows:

```
var i int;
for i=0; i < 5; i++{
  fmt.Printf("I'm in the %d iteration\n", i);
}//end for loop
```

And the output of the above program is as follows:

```
johnbaugh@ubuntu:~/Desktop/go_programming/for_loop$ ./6.out
I'm in the 0 iteration
I'm in the 1 iteration
I'm in the 2 iteration
I'm in the 3 iteration
I'm in the 4 iteration
```

93

Another way to use the `for` loop is by treating it like a `while` loop, leaving out the header and replacing it with semicolons (or nothing, as well shall see). To break out of the loop, the `break` statement can be used.

```
1    package main;
2    import(
3      "fmt"
4    )
5
6    func main(){
7
8      var i int = 5;
9
10     for ; ; {
11       i = i -1;
12       fmt.Printf("The variable i is now : %d\n", i);
13       if i < 0 {
14         break;
15       }
16     }//end for
17   }
```

And the output is as follows:

```
johnbaugh@ubuntu:~/Desktop/go_programming/for_event$ ./6.ou
t
The variable i is now : 4
The variable i is now : 3
The variable i is now : 2
The variable i is now : 1
The variable i is now : 0
The variable i is now : -1
```

In this code, the magic happens on line 10, the `for` loop header. Notice there is no condition check (or anything else for that matter). When there is a condition check missing in Go `for` loops, it defaults to `true`.

This can also be written without a header at all. Instead of:

```
for ; ; {
```

94

You can write:

```
for {
```

The only difference is that we remove the semicolons completely. These types of `for` loops would be infinite loops without the `break` statement.

4.3 break, continue, and Labels

In this section, we will explore some of the more interesting aspects of the `break` and `continue` keywords in Go, including the use of labels.

We have already seen that the `break` statement allows us to break out of a particular block of code, such as a `for` loop. For now, let's look at the `continue` statement.

4.3.1 continue

The `continue` statement causes the current iteration to cease, causing the next iteration of the loop to occur. Let's consider one scenario in which we could print out only the odd numbers in a sequence:

```
1    package main
2    import(
3      "fmt"
4    )
5
6    func main(){
7
8        for i:=0; i<10; i++{
9            if i%2 == 0{
10               continue;
```

```
11          }
12          fmt.Printf("i = %d\n", i);
13      }//end for
14  }
```

And the output of the code is:

```
johnbaugh@ubuntu:~/Desktop/go_programming/continue_example$
./6.out
i = 1
i = 3
i = 5
i = 7
i = 9
```

The meat of the code starts at line 8, where we have our
for loop header. Notice that we are iterating from 0 to 9.
On line 9, we have an interesting condition that you may or
may not be familiar with. If you recall from earlier, I listed
some of the operators in the Go language.

Like C/C++, Go has the *modulus* operator, %. This is also
called the *remainder operator* because it returns the
remainder of the division of the first operand by the second.
For example:

5%2 (read as "5 mod 2" or "5 modulus 2") is equal to 1,
because 5/2 = 2 with a remainder of 1.

In our code, the condition for the if statement on lines 9-11
says, "If the remainder of dividing i by 2 is equal to 0,
execute the continue statement". What does it mean if an
integer divided by 2 has 0 as its remainder? This means the
integer in question is *even*, since all even numbers are, by
definition, divisible by 2 with no remainder.

So, our code, on line 10 specifies that we should continue,
meaning we should skip the rest of the loop body (which
includes the Printf() statement) and go to the next
iteration.

At its highest level, this code says we should skip all the even numbers, and print out all the odd numbers. And, as expected, this is what we see in the output of the program.

4.3.2 *break*

The break statement causes the flow of execution to break out of the innermost construct (such as a for or switch statement). We've seen examples of how break works, earlier in this chapter. Consider the code we saw earlier:

```
1   package main;
2   import(
3     "fmt"
4   )
5
6   func main(){
7
8      var i int = 5;
9
10     for ; ; {
11       i = i -1;
12       fmt.Printf("The variable i is now : %d\n", i);
13       if i < 0 {
14         break;
15       }
16     }//end for
17   }
```

Here, line 14 causes us to break out of the innermost structure (in this case, a for loop). Note that the for loop would be infinite if we did not provide the break to allow a way out.

4.3.3 Labels

Labels are an interesting feature that you should at least be aware of, even though, like goto statements (which we will

97

not cover in this book) can lead to poor program design if not used very carefully.

We could consider an example in which we have embedded for loops:

```
1    package main
2    import(
3      "fmt"
4    )
5
6    func main(){
7
8        myLabel: for i:=0; i < 5; i++{
9          for j:=0; j < 5; j++{
10             if j == 4{
11                continue myLabel;
12             }
13             fmt.Printf("i is : %d, and j is : %d\n", i,j);
14          }
15     }//outer for
16   }
```

And the output:

```
johnbaugh@ubuntu:~/Desktop/go_programming/labels$ ./6.out
i is : 0, and j is : 0
i is : 0, and j is : 1
i is : 0, and j is : 2
i is : 0, and j is : 3
i is : 1, and j is : 0
i is : 1, and j is : 1
i is : 1, and j is : 2
i is : 1, and j is : 3
i is : 2, and j is : 0
i is : 2, and j is : 1
i is : 2, and j is : 2
i is : 2, and j is : 3
i is : 3, and j is : 0
i is : 3, and j is : 1
i is : 3, and j is : 2
i is : 3, and j is : 3
i is : 4, and j is : 0
i is : 4, and j is : 1
i is : 4, and j is : 2
i is : 4, and j is : 3
```

As we can see from the output, even though `j` does equal 4 at different points in the code (five times to be exact), "j is : 4" is never printed out. This is due to lines 10-12. Notice that if `j` is ever equal to 4, we continue to the label `myLabel`, which points to the header of the *outer* `for` loop, which starts `i` at its next value, causing the `j` in the inner `for` loop to reset to 0 (at its initialization).

Note that you can also use a `break` statement with a label, which essentially does the same thing as `continue` with a label. Both are a means by which we jump to a different spot in the code, breaking the current flow of execution.

4.4   Functions

One of the most powerful constructs in Go, and arguably most other high level languages, is the *function*. Functions allow us to break a large problem into smaller tasks. These functions are *called*, or *invoked* and perform the tasks specified by a program.

If you are familiar with functions already, most of this section will be straightforward. However, just like with many other constructs in Go, the syntax is often very different from what you might be accustomed to.

Additionally, Go has a very interesting (and incredibly helpful) approach to allowing us to retrieve multiple return values from the function. The way functions are treated in Go is one of the most interesting treatments of familiar programming constructs that this modern programming language has to offer.

4.4.1   *Single Return Value*

Some functions only return a single value. In this case, the format of the function is as follows:

```
func Identifier(parameter_list) return_type{

}
```

The keyword `func` introduces the header to a function, just like `var` introduces a variable. The parameter_list will consist of parameters, separated by commas, each in the form:

```
paramIdentifier dataType
```

The return type will be the data type of the value that the function returns.

As usual, it is most helpful to look at a concrete example in order to get a better grasp of this concept.

```
1    package main
2    import(
3      "fmt"
4    )
5
6    func main(){
7
8      fmt.Printf("Multiple 2 * 5 * 6 = %d\n",
     Multiply3Nums(2,5,6));
9    }
10
11   func Multiply3Nums(a int, b int, c int) int{
12     return a * b * c;
13   }
```

And the output of the above program is:

```
johnbaugh@ubuntu:~/Desktop/go_programming/func1$ ./6.out
Multiple 2 * 5 * 6 = 60
```

For those unfamiliar with functions, the idea is that we can take a task, such as multiplying three numbers, and give this task (or set of tasks) a name. That way, if we wanted to, we could call this function several times, and not have to rewrite the code in each scenario.

The task of multiplying three numbers is fairly trivial, and the function `Multiply3Nums()` serves to simply educate us on how functions work. On line 11, we have the function header, and on lines 11-13, we have the body of the function.

The header of the function starts with the keyword `func`, then the identifier of the function, `Multiply3Nums` and then the parameter list in parentheses, `(a int, b int, c int)`. Finally, the last thing in the header (before the open curly brace, starting the body of the function) is the return type of the function, which in this case, is `int`.

In the body of the function, we have the value of the three parameters multiplied by one another being returned. Noticed, another way to do this would have been to declare a separate variable, named say, `total`. Then, we would set that variable to the value of the three parameters multiplied by one another, and then return `total`, thusly:

```
...
total = a * b * c;
return total;
...
```

However, this takes an extra variable, adds unnecessary code, and doesn't really add to the readability of the program.

101

In line 8 of our program is the actual *function invocation* (also called the *function call*). While we defined our function on lines 11-13, the function doesn't do anything until we call it from another function, which in this case is the `main()` function. On line 8, we call the function from within the `Printf()` statement. For readability or stylistic reasons, you could choose to separate the function call from the printing of the value by creating a separate variable, such as the following:

```
var myValue int = Multiply3Nums(2,5,6));
fmt.Printf("Multiple 2 * 5 * 6 = %d\n", myValue);
```

But again, I chose not to use a separate variable to store this value, since we are using it immediately, in the `Printf()` function.

We will see more practical and complicated examples of functions as we explore the rest of this section.

4.4.2   Multiple Return Values

One of the more interesting features of functions in Go is that they can return multiple values. A function that returns multiple values is of the form:

```
func functionName(param_list) (return_value_list){
    // function body here
}
```

The `func` keyword begins a function definition, as before. Then, the function identifier `functionName` is after the `func` keyword. Then, as usual, the parameter list `param_list` is inside parentheses. Finally, the primary difference with the multiple return value functions is with the `return_value_list` inside a set of parentheses. With single return value functions, the parentheses are not present and only one return type is specified. In this case, multiple return value types can be specified.

Let's consider a program that contains a function to return multiple values:

```
1    package main
2    import(
3      "fmt"
4    )
5
6    func main(){
7
8        var myNum int = 10;
9        var twiceMyNum int;
10       var thriceMyNum int;
11
12       twiceMyNum, thriceMyNum = getTwiceAndThrice(myNum);
13
14       fmt.Printf("My num is : %d\n", myNum);
15       fmt.Printf("Twice my num : %d\n", twiceMyNum);
16       fmt.Printf("Three times my num :%d\n", thriceMyNum);
17   }
18
19   func getTwiceAndThrice(input int)(int, int){
20
21        return input*2, input*3;   //return twice, and 3
     times the input
22   }
```

And the output of the program is:

```
johnbaugh@ubuntu:~/Desktop/go_programming/multivaluefunc$ .
/6.out
My num is : 10
Twice my num : 20
Three times my num :30
```

On line 8 of this program, we declare our variable to hold the input value, myNum. This integer variable is initialized to the value 10. On lines 9-10, we have two integers to hold the return values from the function, twiceMyNum to hold twice the input value and thriceMyNum to hold three times the input value.

Line 12 is where the function call (or function invocation) occurs. The syntax may seem a little bit peculiar for individuals coming from other languages. In Go, we can perform multiple value assignments in a single line. The variables on the left (`twiceMyNum, thriceMyNum`) match up with the two return values that will be returned by `getTwiceAndThrice()` on the right side of the assignment, respectively.

Finally, in the main function, we perform a print of each of the values on lines 14-16.

Now, we see something new (to us) on lines 19-22. Prior to this, we have defined our own single return value function, but this is the first multiple return value function we have defined.

On line 19, the function header is the same as a single return value function, up to the parameter list. After this, however, we have a set of parentheses with two data types specified, `(int, int)`. In this case, we will have two integer values returned by the function, which we do on line 21.

Notice the `return` statement on line 21. The return values `input*2` and `input*3` will correspond with the first `int` and second `int` in the function header return value list.

There are other possible forms of a multiple return value function, as follows.

Result Parameters

One other form of the multiple return value functions are functions with *result parameters*. In this form, we give names the return value list. Consider our function from earlier:

```
func getTwiceAndThrice(input int)(twoTimes int,threeTimes
int){

    twoTimes = input * 2;
    threeTimes = input * 3;
    return twoTimes, threeTimes;
}
```

Everything in the main function of our program can remain exactly the same as before. But the changes to our getTwiceAndThrice() function are made. In this case, notice that the list of return values has identifiers for the return values. And, inside the body of the function, these values are set as if they were local variables, and returned by name.

Empty Return

Another useful form of the multiple return value function is a function with an empty return.

```
func getTwiceAndThrice(input int)(twoTimes int,threeTimes
int){

    twoTimes = input * 2;
    threeTimes = input * 3;
    return;
}
```

Notice that the return statement is by itself. This will return the value of the result parameters when the return statement is made. In other words, whatever the value of the result parameters when the return statement is made will be the values returned by the function.

4.4.3   The defer Keyword

A helpful keyword that Go makes available to us is defer. This keyword, as the name suggests, allows us to defer the execution of a function until the end of the enclosing function.

Like many programming concepts, this is most easily explained using an example:

```
1    package main
2    import(
3      "fmt"
4    )
5
6    func main(){
7
8        SomeFunction();
9    }
10
11   func DeferredFunc(){
12       fmt.Printf("I was deferred until the end of my
     calling function\n");
13   }
14
15   func SomeFunction(){
16       fmt.Printf("I'm in SomeFunction() at the top\n");
17       defer DeferredFunc();
18       fmt.Printf("I'm now at the bottom of
     SomeFunction()\n");
19   }
```

And the output of the program is:

```
johnbaugh@ubuntu:~/Desktop/go_programming/defer$ ./6.out
I'm in SomeFunction() at the top
I'm now at the bottom of SomeFunction()
I was deferred until the end of my calling function
```

In the main function, on line 8, we call SomeFunction(). Since SomeFunction() has no return values, we do not have to capture any values. It is a special type of function, just like main(), that performs a set of tasks and simply exits when it completes. This is analogous to `void` functions in languages like C/C++.

The first function we define after `main()` is `DeferedFunc()`, which, like `SomeFunction()` does not return a value. On line 12, all it does is print some information before exiting.

Lines 15-19 make up the body of `SomeFunction()`. On line 16, we print a statement indicating that we're at the top of `SomeFunction()`. Then, on line 17, we call `defer` on our `DeferedFunc()` function, and finally on line 18, we print another statement, indicating we're at the bottom of `SomeFunction()`.

Pay careful attention to the output of the program. Notice that the print statement in our deferred function is not performed until *after* the two print statements that are present in `SomeFunction()`, even though it was called in between these two print statements.

Remove the `defer` statement, and the order will be different. The `defer` keyword allows us to ensure that certain tasks are performed before we return from a function. It can be helpful to keep the code itself clean, as well as to ensure certain tasks such as closing a file stream.

4.4.4   The Blank Identifier

In this subsection, we learn about the *blank identifier*, which is denoted by an underscore, _. The blank identifier is helpful when we have a multiple return value function, but do not want to store all of the values it returns.

In Go, it is a syntax error to not capture all of the return values of a function. If we capture a value, we must then use it, and this gets clumsy and makes the code messy with variables we don't really intend on using. So, the blank identifier comes to the rescue.

Consider the following:

```
1    package main
2    import(
3        "fmt"
4    )
5
6    func main(){
7        var myInteger int;
8        var myFloat float;
9
10       myInteger,_, myFloat = ThreeValues();
11
12       fmt.Printf("My int : %d, my float : %f\n",
         myInteger, myFloat);
13   }
14
15   func ThreeValues() (int, int, float){
16       return 5, 6, 7.5;
17   }
```

And the output is:

```
johnbaugh@ubuntu:~/Desktop/go_programming/blankidentifier$
./6.out
My int : 5, my float : 7.500000
```

In this program, we have defined a trivial function named ThreeValues() in order to demonstrate how the blank identifier works. The function returns the values 5, 6, and 7.5. In our main() function, we are simply wishing to capture the first int and the float value, ignoring the integer return value in the middle (in our case, 6).

So, on line 10, we use our declared myInteger to capture the first integer return value, then we use the blank identifier to capture and drop the second integer return value, and then we capture the third return value, which is a float, in our myFloat variable.

4.4.5   Example : Minimum / Maximum Function

To further enhance our understanding of functions, I will give a simple example of a function that returns the minimum and maximum of two integers.

The code:

```
1    package main
2    import(
3      "fmt"
4    )
5
6    func main(){
7        var myMax int;
8        var myMin int;
9        myMax,myMin = MinMax(10,15);
10       fmt.Printf("Min : %d\nMax: %d\n", myMin, myMax);
11   }
12   func MinMax(a int, b int)(max int, min int){
13
14       if a < b {
15          min = a;
16          max = b;
17       }else {
18          min = b;
19          max = a;
20       }
21
22       return max, min;
23   }
```

The output:

```
johnbaugh@ubuntu:~/Desktop/go_programming/minmax$ ./6.out
Min : 10
Max: 15
```

109

The `MinMax()` function is quite simple. It just assigns the minimum and maximum value and returns them in the order of maximum, then minimum.

4.4   Summary

In this chapter, we've explored control structures and functions.

We learned about conditional (also known as *branching*) control structures, such as `if-else` and `switch` structures. We also learned about the only iterative (also known as *looping*) control structure, the `for` structure.

Furthermore, we learned about functions, and how to use them to break a larger problem into smaller, more manageable sub-problems. Functions allow us to perform a task or set of tasks over and over again (if we wish), without having to write the same code over and over again. In Go, we can have functions that return no value, one value, or multiple values.

Chapter 5

More Data Types

In this chapter, we will explore some more of the data types that Go has to offer. We will look at several composite structures available in Go, including arrays, slices, and maps.

We will begin with *arrays*, commonly available structures that are used in many programming languages for storing homogenous groups of data. However, we will see that arrays in Go are significantly different from arrays in many other high level languages.

Additionally, we will explore the *slice* structure, which is a *reference* to a section of an array, and more accurately approximates what readers from other programming languages expect from an array.

Also, we will explore *maps*, which are associate arrays.

Inherent to the discussion of these data types is understanding *pointers*, which we will investigate first.

5.1   Pointers and References

Computers store values in memory, and each memory block has an address. A *pointer* is a special data type in which the *memory address* of another value is stored. Thus, a pointer points to the location of another value.

Related directly to pointers is the *address-of* operator, denoted by the ampersand, &, which is used to determine the address of a particular piece of data. Let's consider the following example:

```
1   package main
2   import(
3     "fmt"
4   )
5
6   func main(){
7     var someInt int = 5;
8
9     fmt.Printf("My integer: %d.  Its location in memory:
    %p\n", someInt, &someInt);
10  }
```

And the output is:

```
johnbaugh@ubuntu:~/Desktop/go_programming/chap5/pointers$ .
/6.out
My integer: 5.  Its location in memory: 0x7F6927B25010
```

On line 7, we simply declare an integer variable, and set its value to 5. Line 9 is where we get to see the address-of operator in action. As we see from the output, the first piece of data we print out is 5, which is contained in our variable, someInt. Next, we print out the value 0x7F6927B25010, which is the address returned by &someInt.

Note that this value is hexadecimal (base-16) and that the actual address value of the memory location is after the 0x part. 0x denotes that the number following is in base-16. Also note that this value will change when you run the program more than once. This is because the memory location assigned to the variable changes with distinct executions of the program.

What if we wanted to store the address of a piece of data into a variable, rather than just use it directly like we did in the code above? No problem. That's where pointers come in. To declare a pointer, we put an asterisk, *, in front of the data type we are pointing to.

Let's consider the following example, which is a modification of the above code:

```
1    package main
2    import(
3      "fmt"
4    )
5
6    func main(){
7      var someInt int = 5;
8      var intPtr *int;
9
10     intPtr = &someInt;
11
12     fmt.Printf("My integer: %d.   Its location in memory:
       %p\n", someInt, &someInt);
13     fmt.Printf("The value at memory location %p is :
       %d\n", intPtr, *intPtr);
14   }
```

And the output is:

```
johnbaugh@ubuntu:~/Desktop/go_programming/chap5/pointers$ .
/6.out
My integer: 5.   Its location in memory: 0x7FBF3AF8C010
The value at memory location 0x7FBF3AF8C010 is : 5
```

In this example, on line 8, we declare a pointer variable, intPtr. Note the type of this variable is *int, which means "pointer to an integer". On line 10, we set the value of intPtr to the address of someInt using the address-of operator.

I've left line 12 the same so that we can make a comparison. Line 13 is where a couple new things appear. Notice that the variable `intPtr`, when printed out, is equal to the `&someInt` from the previous `Printf()`, which is expected since `intPtr` contains the address of `someInt`.

At the end of line 13, however, we have some syntax that may look unfamiliar to those who have not worked with a high level programming language that allows pointer manipulation, like C/C++, or Go. Notice the statement `*intPtr`.

In this case, when the asterisk is in front of a variable that is a pointer, it is referred to as the *pointer dereference operator* or just the *dereference operator* for short. It takes a pointer as its operand and asks the pointer, "What value are you pointing to?".

As we can see from the output, when we ask the pointer, "What are you pointing to?", we get, not surprisingly, the data stored in `someInt` (namely, the value 5), since `intPtr` is pointing to `someInt`.

5.2   Arrays and Slices

In this section, we will explore *arrays* and *slices*, two composite types that can contain multiple values. We will first consider arrays in Go, and then slices, which are actually more similar to arrays from other high level languages than the actual array type in Go.

5.2.1   Arrays

Arrays are defined to be a *numbered sequence of homogenous data elements*. By homogeneous, I mean that the data contained in an array must be of a single data type, (such as integers, strings, Booleans, etc.) known as the *element type*. You can think of an array as a long box with different compartments in it, with each being able to contain a piece of data.

To declare an array in Go, you use the following form:

```
[numElements]dataType identifier
```

where `numElements` is the number of items the array can hold, called the *length*. Also, `dataType` is the type of data to be stored in the array, and `identifier` is of course, the name of the array.

Arrays in Go are *values*, not pointers like they are in languages like C/C++. So, when you assign one array to another, a distinct copy of the array is made.

Another important feature of arrays in Go is that their length is part of their data type.

Thus:

```
[5]int
```

is a distinct data type from

```
[10]int
```

even though they both contain integers.

Let's consider an example that makes use of arrays:

```
1    package main
```

```
2    import(
3      "fmt"
4    )
5
6    func main(){
7      var myArray [5]int;
8
9      for i:=0; i < len(myArray); i++{
10         myArray[i] = i * 2;
11     }//end for
12
13     for j:=0; j < len(myArray); j++{
14         fmt.Printf("Array at %d is %d\n", j, myArray[j]);
15     }//end for
16   }
```

And the output is:

```
johnbaugh@ubuntu:~/Desktop/go_programming/chap5/arrays$ ./6
.out
Array at 0 is 0
Array at 1 is 2
Array at 2 is 4
Array at 3 is 6
Array at 4 is 8
```

In this program, we declare an array that can hold 5 integers on line 7, called myArray. On lines 9-11 we make use of a for loop to store data in the array. Interestingly, on line 9, we use len(), which is a compile-time constant that returns the length of the array.

Line 10 is fairly self explanatory. Arrays are *zero-indexed,* meaning that their first index starts at 0, and the last index of an array is one less than the array length (i.e., len(array)-1). With each iteration of the loop, the value stored in that *index* (like an individual compartment in a box) is set to twice the value of the index, i.

Lines 13-15 are responsible for printing out the value stored within each location within the array.

An important note is that the value at each index of the array is automatically set to 0.

Array literals are another way to use arrays. Let's consider a larger example to see some of the usefulness of array literals:

```
1   package main
2   import(
3     "fmt"
4   )
5
6   func main(){
7     var ageArray = [5]int{18,20,15,22,16};
8     var lazyArray = [...]int{5,6,7,8,22};
9     var keyValueArray = [5]string{3:"John", 4:"George"};
10
11    for i:=0; i < len(ageArray); i++{
12      fmt.Printf("Age at %d is : %d\n", i, ageArray[i]);
13    }//end for
14
15    fmt.Printf("\n");
16
17    for j:=0; j<len(lazyArray); j++{
18      fmt.Printf("Int at %d is : %d\n", j, lazyArray[j]);
19    }//end for
20
21    fmt.Printf("\n");
22
23    for k:=0; k<len(keyValueArray); k++{
24      fmt.Printf("Name at : %d is : %s\n", k,
      keyValueArray[k]);
25    }//end for
26  }
```

And the output is:

```
johnbaugh@ubuntu:~/Desktop/go_programming/chap5/array_liter
als$ ./6.out
Age at 0 is : 18
Age at 1 is : 20
Age at 2 is : 15
Age at 3 is : 22
Age at 4 is : 16

Int at 0 is : 5
```

```
Int at 1 is : 6
Int at 2 is : 7
Int at 3 is : 8
Int at 4 is : 22

Name at : 0 is :
Name at : 1 is :
Name at : 2 is :
Name at : 3 is : John
Name at : 4 is : George
```

This example has a lot going on. We have three arrays that we are dealing with in this case. Notice the not-so-typical syntax we use when declaring on lines 7-9. First, notice that I don't put the data type on the same side as the identifier. While you *can* put the data type on that side as well, such as in:

```
var ageArray [5]int = [5]int{18,20,15,22,16};
```

this is generally seen as overly verbose. But, if you wish, you may use this syntax.

The most interesting of these declarations is on line 8, with our variable `lazyArray`. In this case, we use ... as the size of the array. This will automatically determine the length of the array based on the number of elements, so we don't have to explicitly indicate it.

However, note that you *cannot* do the following:

```
var lazyArray [...]int = [...]int{5,6,7,8,22};
```

This will raise a syntax error. The ... must only be used in the context of a literal, not as a data type in the declaration of the variable itself, whereas a specific integer (such as `[5]`) can be used in either declarations or literals.

The declaration on line 9 uses *key value* syntax. When an array is declared, if the values are not set explicitly, the zero value of whatever type is being stored (i.e., 0 for `int`, 0.0 for `float`, the empty string for `strings`) is set. But, if we want to initialize certain values explicitly and not others, we can use key-value syntax, with the following form:

```
key:value
```

In our example, on line 9, `3:"John"` means "Store the string *John* at index 3".

Additionally, it is important to remember that arrays in Go are *values*, not *pointers*, as they are in C/C++. So, when you pass an array to a function:

```
myFunc(myArray);
```

a copy of the array is made. To pass it by reference (in other words, by the memory address of the array), you use the address-of operator, `&`:

```
someFunction(&myArray);
```

5.2.2   Slices

A *slice* is a reference to a section of an array. This section may be the entire array, or a subset of the various indices of the array. Because slices are references, they are less expensive to use than arrays, and are therefore used more often than arrays. Additionally, unlike an array, the length of a slice can change during execution of the code.

The declaration of a slice is like that of an array, except without the size, as follows:

```
var mySlice [] int;
```

A slice that has not yet been initialized is set to `nil` by default, and has 0 length.

Two important functions related to slices are:

```
len(mySlice);
```

```
cap(mySlice);
```

The function `len()` returns the length of the slice itself (how many elements are in the slice), whereas the `cap()` function returns the sum of the length of the slice and the number of elements from the end of the slice, to the end of the underlying array.

Basic Usage

Let's consider a basic scenario where a slice is used:

```
1    package main
2    import(
3      "fmt"
4    )
5
6    func main(){
7        var myArray [6]int;
8        var mySlice []int = myArray[2:5];
9
10       //load the array
11       for i:=0; i<len(myArray); i++{
12         myArray[i] = i;
13       }
14
15       //print the slice
16       for i:=0; i<len(mySlice); i++{
17          fmt.Printf("Slice at : %d is %d\n", i,
      mySlice[i]);
18       }
19
20       fmt.Printf("Length of myArray is : %d\n",
      len(myArray));
21       fmt.Printf("Length of mySlice is : %d\n",
```

```
      len(mySlice));
22        fmt.Printf("Capacity of mySlice is: %d\n",
      cap(mySlice));
23    }
```

The output looks like:

```
johnbaugh@ubuntu:~/Desktop/go_programming/chap5/basic_slice
$ ./6.out
Slice at : 0 is 2
Slice at : 1 is 3
Slice at : 2 is 4
Length of myArray is : 6
Length of mySlice is : 3
Capacity of mySlice is: 4
```

In this program, we declare an array on line 7 called myArray, that holds 6 integers. On line 8, we create a slice of myArray called mySlice. The slice contains the elements at indices 2, 3, and 4 from the original array.

Note that since the slice is a reference to the underlying array, that we declared the reference earlier than when we populated the array on lines 11-13.

Near the bottom, on lines 20-22, we print the lengths of myArray and mySlice, and the capacity of mySlice.

Using make() to Create a Slice

While the above example is a perfectly acceptable usage of slices, it is not always the case that we will have an array already defined to reference.

Sometimes, we want to create a slice and an underlying array, without an array being previously defined. In this case, we must use the function make().

Let's consider an example:

121

```
1    package main
2    import(
3      "fmt"
4    )
5
6    func main(){
7      var newSlice []int = make([]int, 10);
8
9      for i:=0; i<len(newSlice); i++{
10         newSlice[i] = 5 * i;
11       }//end for
12
13       for j:=0; j<len(newSlice); j++{
14         fmt.Printf("Slice at %d is %d\n",j, newSlice[j]);
15       }//end for
16     }
```

And the output is:

```
johnbaugh@ubuntu:~/Desktop/go_programming/chap5/make_slice$
./6.out
Slice at 0 is 0
Slice at 1 is 5
Slice at 2 is 10
Slice at 3 is 15
Slice at 4 is 20
Slice at 5 is 25
Slice at 6 is 30
Slice at 7 is 35
Slice at 8 is 40
Slice at 9 is 45
```

In this program, we use the make() function to create a slice of integers. The function make() is used to create slices, maps, and channels, which we will see later.

On line 7, notice that the make() function takes two parameters. The first, []int in our case, is the data type that is to be created. The second parameter, the number 10 in our example, indicates that number of items to be in the slice.

This code creates an array, and then automatically creates a slice referencing the array. The remainder of the program

122

is fairly self-explanatory. Lines 9-11 are responsible for filling the slice (or the underlying array, to be exact) with values. And then, on lines 13-15, the values are printed.

Reslicing

Another useful form of the make() function involves not two, but three parameters. The basic format of this version of make() is:

```
make(data_type, starting_length, capacity)
```

The parameter data_type is (not surprisingly) the data type of the array in question (such as []int). The starting_length is the beginning length of the slice, and the capacity is the entire length of the underlying array.

Since slices have the ability to grow within the limits of the underlying array, it may be useful to create a slice that is smaller than the underlying array, but can also grow as needed when elements are added.

In the following example, we can see how resizing of the slice is done:

```
1    package main
2    import(
3      "fmt"
4    )
5
6    func main(){
7      var slice1 []int = make([]int, 0, 10);
8      var numElements int = 0;
9
10     for i:=0; i < cap(slice1); i++{
11       slice1 = slice1[0:numElements+1]; //reslice
12       slice1[i] = i;
13       numElements = numElements + 1;
14       fmt.Printf("Length of slice is : %d\n",
       len(slice1));
```

123

```
15    } //end for i
16
17    for j:=0; j < len(slice1); j++{
18       fmt.Printf("Slice at : %d is %d\n", j, slice1[j]);
19    } //end for j
20
21  }
```

Here is the output:

```
johnbaugh@ubuntu:~/Desktop/go_programming/chap5/resize_slic
e$ ./6.out
Length of slice is : 1
Length of slice is : 2
Length of slice is : 3
Length of slice is : 4
Length of slice is : 5
Length of slice is : 6
Length of slice is : 7
Length of slice is : 8
Length of slice is : 9
Length of slice is : 10
Slice at : 0 is 0
Slice at : 1 is 1
Slice at : 2 is 2
Slice at : 3 is 3
Slice at : 4 is 4
Slice at : 5 is 5
Slice at : 6 is 6
Slice at : 7 is 7
Slice at : 8 is 8
Slice at : 9 is 9
```

On line 7 of the code, we make an integer slice starting
with zero length, but with an underlying array that has a
capacity of 10. On line 8, we declare numElements, which
will serve as the counter of the number of elements in the
slice (note that we could creatively use the variable i for
this purpose, but I want to make it more clear what is going
on in the code).

Lines 10-15 contain the loop that fills the slice with data.
Line 11 is of particular interest, however, because we
"reslice" the slice, adding one to its length. The loop itself
prevents us from going out of bounds on the underlying
capacity, so we don't need to check for this. Note in the

output, that the length of the slice keeps increasing with each iteration of the loop.

On lines 17-19, we have the loop that allows us to print the contents of the slice. Note for this loop, we can use the `len()` function for the loop condition.

As a final note about slices, the growing ability of a slice would be more useful, not in a strictly iterating structure like a loop, but if it were for the purpose of retrieving input from say, the user. It would be a typical case that we would have no knowledge of exactly how many integers the user was going to enter. As long as it was within the capacity, the user could enter 0 or more data elements.

5.3   Maps

Maps in Go are essentially *associative arrays*. They are similar to `*map<string, float>` in C++ or the `dict` (dictionary) type in Python. With maps, you can associate (hence why they're called *associative arrays*) a *key* with a value, called the *data* or just the *value*.

Maps are an alternative to strict arrays or slices, which use integers as indices. Instead, you can use a value of any data type for the index for which `==` and `!=` are defined to find a particular piece of data. For example, the data type `string` can be used as the key type since `==` and `!=` are defined for `strings`.

Let's consider an example:

```
1    package main
2    import(
3      "fmt"
4    )
```

```
5
6    func main(){
7      var myMapLiteral map[string] int;
8      var myMapCreated map[string] float;
9      var myMapAssigned map[string] int;
10
11     myMapLiteral = map[string] int { "one":1, "two":2 };
12     myMapCreated = make(map[string]float);
13     myMapAssigned = myMapLiteral;
14
15     myMapCreated["chicken"] = 4.5;
16     myMapCreated["pi"] = 3.14159;
17
18     fmt.Printf("Map Literal at \"one\" is : %d\n",
       myMapLiteral["one"]);
19
20     fmt.Printf("Map Created at \"chicken\" is : %f\n",
       myMapCreated["chicken"]);
21
22     fmt.Printf("Map Assigned at \"two\" is : %d\n",
       myMapAssigned["two"]);
23
24
25   }
```

And the output is:

```
johnbaugh@ubuntu:~/Desktop/go_programming/chap5/maps$ ./6.o
ut
Map Literal at "one" is : 1
Map Created at "chicken" is : 4.500000
Map Assigned at "two" is : 2
```

This example shows three different ways of creating an
instance of a map type. On line 7, we declare a map,
myMapLiteral that is indexed with keys of type string,
and contains ints. This map is populated with literals on
line 11, using key-value pairs inside curly braces.

On line 8, we declare a map called myMapCreated which
has keys of type string and contains float values. We
create and populate this map in a slightly different way. We
actually create a map on line 12 with the make() function.

126

It is interesting to note that `maps` automatically grow to accommodate any key-values that are added. You can, however, optionally `make()` the `map` with a starting capacity:

```
make(map[string] float, 50)
```

would create a `map` that uses `string`s as the key and `float`s as the value type, with an initial capacity of 50. As mentioned, this will not limit the size of the `map`. When the number of values reaches 50, the next key-value added will cause the `map` to increase its size by 1 automatically.

Line 9 creates a `map` named `myMapAssigned`, which is assigned to refer to `myMapLiteral` on line 13. Since `myMapAssigned` now refers to the same `map` as `myMapLiteral`, we can use it as if it *were* `myMapLiteral`, by using the same indices.

For the `map` that was created, we assign it values on lines 15 and 16. We can see how `map`s work from the output, which is performed on lines 18-22. As mentioned above, pay close attention to line 22. We can use `myMapAssigned["two"]` because `myMapAssigned` refers to the same `map` as `myMapLiteral`, which has an index named "two".

Testing for Existence of an Element

Sometimes, we want to know if an item exists in a `map`. In order to do this, we use the following so-called *comma ok* form to test for the existence of an element:

```
value, isPresent = someMap[key]
```

The variable `value` will contain the value at the key in question if it exists. If the key is not present in the `map`, then the value returned will be the zero-value for that particular data type (0 for `int`, 0.0 for `float`, etc.)

The variable `isPresent` will always be of type `boolean` and is `true` if the key is present in the `map`, or `false` if it is not present.

Deleting an Element

It is a common task to delete an element from a map. Essentially, we use the *comma ok* form in reverse:

```
someMap[key] = value, delete
```

In the above expression, `value` can be essentially anything, and `delete` is a `boolean` value that you should set to `false` if you wish to delete a value of a particular `key`.

As an example of deleting elements, and testing for the existence of particular key-value pairs, let's consider the following code:

```
1    package main
2    import(
3      "fmt"
4    )
5
6    func main(){
7      var myMap map[string]int;
8      var value int;
9      var isPresent bool;
10
11     myMap = make(map[string]int);
12
13     myMap["horses"] = 55;
14     myMap["cows"] = 20;
15     myMap["pigs"] = 25;
16
```

```
17      value, isPresent = myMap["horses"];
18      fmt.Printf("Is \"horses\" in myMap? :
    %t\n",isPresent);
19      fmt.Printf("Value is : %d\n", value);
20
21      value, isPresent = myMap["chicken"];
22      fmt.Printf("Is \"chicken\" in myMap? : %t\n",
    isPresent);
23      fmt.Printf("Value is : %d\n", value);
24
25      //delete an item
26      myMap["horses"] = 0,false;
27      value, isPresent = myMap["horses"];
28      fmt.Printf("Is \"horses\" in myMap? : %t\n",
    isPresent);
29    }
```

And the output is:

```
johnbaugh@ubuntu:~/Desktop/go_programming/chap5/exist_map$
./6.out
Is "horses" in myMap? : true
Value is : 55
Is "chicken" in myMap? : false
Value is : 0
Is "horses" in myMap? : false
```

Lines 7 - 15 contain the creation (using make()) and the
initialization of our map, myMap. Line 17 tests for the
existence of the key "horses". Since this is in myMap, we
see that isPresent is assigned the value true, and value
is assigned the value 55. These are printed on lines 18-19.

Later, on lines 21-23, we test the existence of the key
"chicken". Since "chicken" does not exist as a key,
isPresent is assigned the value false, and value is
assigned the value 0 (since 0 is the zero-value for integers).

Finally, we delete the value at key "horses" on line 26, by
using the comma ok form with any value as the first value
and false as the second. On line 27, we test for the
existence of the key "horses", which is now false (since
we deleted it). As you can see, the output reflects this.

5.4   Using `range` with `for` Loops

So far in this book, we have explored various composite types such as arrays, slices and `maps`. We also have done some work with `strings`. Up to this point, we have only seen basic `for` loops, but there is another form of the `for` loop that is perfectly suited for `strings` and composite types (and `channels`, but we haven't explored these yet in this book).

This form of the `for` loop is based on the `range` of elements in the composite type (or characters in the `string`).

Let's consider an example using `maps`:

```
1    package main
2    import(
3      "fmt"
4    )
5
6    func main(){
7      var myMap map[int] float;
8      var key int;
9      var value float;
10
11     myMap = make(map[int]float);
12     myMap[1] = 1.0;
13     myMap[2] = 2.0;
14     myMap[3] = 3.0;
15     myMap[4] = 4.0;
16
17     for key,value = range myMap {
18       fmt.Printf("key is : %d\n", key);
19       fmt.Printf("value is : %f\n\n", value);
20     }//end for
21   }
```

And the output is:

```
johnbaugh@ubuntu:~/Desktop/go_programming/chap5/for_r
ange$ ./6.out
key is : 4
value is : 4.000000

key is : 1
value is : 1.000000

key is : 2
value is : 2.000000

key is : 3
value is : 3.000000
```

In this program, we declare a map on line 7 called myMap. The keys in this map are ints, and the values are floats. We create the map using make() on line 11. Then, we populate the indices 1 through 4 with values on lines 12 - 15.

On lines 17 - 20, we use a for loop with the range form to iterate over items in the map. With this form, you must have at least the key, and optionally you may capture the value (which we have in this example).

However, the output is interesting. Notice that the key at index 4 is printed out first. With maps, this order could be anything, because by definition, maps are unordered.

The situation is quite different if we were to use an ordered composite type, such as a slice.

Let's see what happens when we iterate over a slice using the range form of the for loop:

```
1    package main
2    import(
```

```
3      "fmt"
4    )
5
6    func main(){
7        var mySlice []int = make([]int, 4);
8
9        mySlice[0] = 15;
10       mySlice[1] = 20;
11       mySlice[2] = 25;
12       mySlice[3] = 30;
13
14       for key,value := range mySlice {
15           fmt.Printf("Slice at %d is %d\n", key,
     value);
16       }
17   }
```

And the output is:
```
johnbaugh@ubuntu:~/Desktop/go_programming/chap5/for_r
ange$ ./6.out
Slice at 0 is 15
Slice at 1 is 20
Slice at 2 is 25
Slice at 3 is 30
```

Here, we use essentially the same syntax as with `maps`. But, as you can see from the output, the data in the slice is in the order we added it to the slice. This is because arrays and slices are ordered composite types. Note also on line 14, our usage of the idiomatic (quick and easy) `:=` without having declared `key` or `value` previously.

5.5   Simulating Enumerated Types with `iota`

Many readers may be wondering if Go supports anything like the `enum` type of languages like C++. Go does not technically have an enumerated type, but this can be simulated by the `iota` identifier. The `iota` identifier is used in `const` blocks. It resets to 0 any time the keyword `const` is encountered, and increments any time a semicolon is encountered. It therefore represents integer constants in succession.

An example of iota in practice is:

```
1    package main
2    import (
3       "fmt"
4    )
5
6    func main() {
7       const (
8          first = iota;
9          second = iota;
10         third = iota;
11      )
12
13      fmt.Printf("first : %d\n", first);
14      fmt.Printf("second: %d\n", second);
15      fmt.Printf("third: %d\n", third);
16   }
```

The above code has the output:

```
johnbaugh@ubuntu:~/Desktop/go_programming/chap5/iota$
./6.out
first : 0
second: 1
third: 2
```

In the code, notice the `const` block on lines 7-11. Each successive usage of `iota` will increment by 1. This is why the output starts at 0 (since `iota` is set to 0 at the beginning of the `const` block), and ends at 2. We do not have to explicitly include the semicolon at the end of each statement, as Go automatically inserts one. In fact, many Go programmer prefer this way:

```
7    const (
8       first = iota
```

```
9        second
10       third
11    )
```

With this syntax, we leave out the semicolons. Additionally, notice we do not have to keep using = iota after every const identifier. Go will automatically use the last assignment if none is explicitly written.

Note that if we wanted to start our enumeration at say, 50, we could use iota+50 with the initialization of the elements.

5.6   Summary

In this chapter, we enhanced our knowledge of Go by exploring more of the data types that the language has to offer. We began the chapter discussing reference types and pointers, and learned how they represent memory addresses of other types.

We also focused on the composite types, including arrays, slices and maps. We learned that slices exist on top of an underlying array. Slices grow as needed, but we can also use make() to give them an initial capacity. The map type represents associative arrays, in which a key-value pair is used. As long as the == and != operators are defined for a particular type, we can use that type as the key.

We explored how we can use range with for loops to iterate over the composite types learned about in this chapter.

Finally, we briefly learned how to simulate enumerated types with the iota identifier.

Chapter 6

Structured Types, Packages and Interfaces

In this chapter, we will look at structured types, interface types, interfaces, the methods to implement interfaces, and the values that are possible for these special types. Go has a somewhat unusual and novel approach to object awareness, and the unique concepts involving interfaces, interface types, and interface values.

6.1   Structured Types

In this section, we'll explore the `struct` keyword, and how we can create specialized groups of information, called struct types, or structured types. It is often helpful to group pieces of data together, and to be able to access that data as if it were part of a single entity. Structured types help us do that.

6.1.1   Named Fields and Anonymous Fields

Structured types contain *fields*, which are the component pieces of data that constitute the structured type. Let's consider an example:

```
1    package main
2    import(
3      "fmt"
4    )
5
6    type myStruct struct{
7        someInteger int;
8        someFloat float;
9        someString string;
10   }
11
12   func main(){
13       var ms *myStruct = new(myStruct);
14
15       ms.someInteger = 10;
16       ms.someFloat = 15.5;
17       ms.someString = "John";
18
19       fmt.Printf("My int is : %d\n", ms.someInteger);
20       fmt.Printf("My float is : %f\n", ms.someFloat);
21       fmt.Printf("My string is : %s\n", ms.someString);
22
23   }
```

And the output is:

```
johnbaugh@ubuntu:~/Desktop/go_programming/chap6$ ./6.out
My int is : 10
My float is : 15.500000
My string is : John
```

On lines 6-9, we declare and define our structured type, myStruct. This structure has three fields, someInteger, someFloat, and someString. This means that whenever we create an instance of this structured type, the instance will have three constituent components with those names.

On line 13, we declare a variable, ms, that is a pointer to an instance of myStruct. This is why we must put the symbol

136

$*$ in front of the data type of the structure. Notice that we then allocate the memory for the structure with the `new()` function.

At this point, the three fields contain the zero values for their respective types. In other words, the `int` contains a 0, the `float`, a 0.0, and the `string`, an empty string, "".

We can now populate the fields using the name of the variable (`ms`) and the dot operator (`.`), followed by the name of the field we wish to assign a value to. For those coming from the C/C++ world, this may seem peculiar.

In C/C++, you must use the *class member access operator* (`->`) to access the members of an object being pointed to. Thus, in C/C++, `objName->fieldName` is equivalent to `(*objName).fieldName`. There is no such class member access operator in Go. The indirection is performed *automatically* with the dot operator.

Thus, we are able to populate `ms` on lines 15-17. On lines 19-21, we print the data stored in `ms` to the console.

Another useful feature of structures in Go is that they can have *anonymous fields*. The fields in the above example are specifically called *named fields*, because, well, the fields have names!

Fields that don't have names may seem a bit peculiar at first. These unnamed fields can even be structs themselves. Although Go does not directly support inheritance in the same way that a language like C++ or Java does, anonymous fields allow for the embedding of the members of the inner struct into the outer struct.

Let's consider some code:

```
1    package main
2    import(
3      "fmt"
4    )
5
6    //inner struct
7    type innerStruct struct{
8        innerInt int;
9        innerInt2 int;
10   }
11
12   //outer struct
13   type outerStruct struct{
14       b int;
15       c float;
16       int;   //anonymous field
17       innerStruct;  //anonymous field
18   }
19
20   func main(){
21
22       var outer *outerStruct = new(outerStruct);
23
24       outer.innerInt = 5;
25       outer.innerInt2 = 10;
26       outer.b = 6;
27       outer.c = 7.5;
28       outer.int = 60;
29
30       fmt.Printf("outer.innerInt = %d\n", outer.innerInt);
31       fmt.Printf("outer.innerInt2 = %d\n",
     outer.innerInt2);
32       fmt.Printf("outer.b = %d\n", outer.b);
33       fmt.Printf("outer.c = %f\n", outer.c);
34       fmt.Printf("outer.int = %d\n", outer.int);
35   }
```

And here is the output:

```
johnbaugh@ubuntu:~/Desktop/go_programming/chap6/anonymous_f
ields$ ./6.out
outer.innerInt = 5
outer.innerInt2 = 10
outer.b = 6
outer.c = 7.500000
outer.int = 60
```

Here, on lines 7-10, we declare and define a structured type called `innerStruct`. Note that it has two integer fields, `innerInt` and `innerInt2`. Later on in the program, we declare and define a second structure on lines 13-18, called `outerStruct`. This structure has named fields, an integer called `b` and a floating point type called `c`.

After these, we then see a couple peculiar things that we haven't dealt with before now. On line 16, we have just a data type listed, `int`. This is an anonymous field. There is no identifier. In fact, when we want to store data in this field or access the data, we simply use the name of the data type. Notice also there would only be the ability to have one anonymous field of each data type. In other words, for example, we could not have two anonymous fields named `int`. This would be a naming conflict.

On line 17, notice that we use another anonymous field. This time, it is the name of a type we've defined elsewhere in the file. Namely, we've embedded `innerStruct` into `outerStruct`. What this does is simply causes any fields of `innerStruct` to be directly accessible from instances of `outerStruct`.

The majority of the rest of the program is fairly self explanatory, with a couple notes. On line 22 we create the instance of `outerStruct` called `outer`. On lines 24-28, we populate the members of `outerStruct`. Notice the first two, `innerInt` and `innerInt2` that come from the `innerStruct`. They are accessed directly from `outer` rather than having to go through another layer of hierarchy, as would likely be the case in another language. In other words:

```
outer.innerStruct.innerInt
```

would be incorrect. Instead, we need to simply use:

```
outer.innerInt
```

to access or assign values.

Lines 30-34 print the values that we stored in the structured type instance, which we can observe from the output.

6.1.2 Methods

Methods in Go have much the same syntax as regular functions, except that they have a *receiver*. The general signature for a method is:

```
func (receiver) FuncName(params) returnType{
// .. body
}
```

The receiver is specified in parentheses *before* the name of the method. A receiver is the type that the method acts upon.

The best way to understand this is to see an example of how methods can act upon a structured type.

```
1    package main
2    import(
3      "fmt"
4    )
5
6    type TwoNums struct{
7      a int;
8      b int;
9    }
10
11   func main(){
12     var myTn *TwoNums; //ptr to instance
13     myTn = new(TwoNums);
14     myTn.a = 12;
15     myTn.b = 10;
```

```
16
17    fmt.Printf("The sum is : %d\n", myTn.AddThem());
18    fmt.Printf("Add them to the param : %d\n",
      myTn.AddToParam(20));
19    }
20
21    func (tn *TwoNums) AddThem() int{
22        return tn.a + tn.b;
23    }
24
25    func (tn *TwoNums) AddToParam(param int) int{
26        return tn.a + tn.b + param;
27    }
28
```

And the output is :

```
johnbaugh@ubuntu:~/Desktop/go_programming/chap6/methods$ ./
6.out
The sum is : 22
Add them to the param : 42
```

Here, we declare a structured type named TwoNums. This structure contains two integer fields, a and b. On lines 12-15, we declare and assign values to the fields of our struct instance, myTn. Now, if you look a little farther down in the file, you will notice two different methods defined on lines 21-27.

The first method, called AddThem() states its receiver as a TwoNums struct. Although we could have just used TwoNums directly, it is more efficient to use pointers, which is why the data type of tn is *TwoNums.

TwoNums is said to be the *receiver base type*, or just *base type*. It is important to note that the receiver base type must be declared within the same package and cannot be a pointer or interface type.

The method AddThem() takes the fields of a TwoNums structure, adds them, and returns them. Notice how they are accessed using the name of the identifier of the receiver. Go does not have an implicit `this` pointer available that languages like Java have. Therefore, you must give the receiver an explicit name. In our case, it is called `tn`.

The second method, `AddToParam` not only adds the fields of the structures, but also adds an additional parameter and returns the sum of all three.

Now, we need to jump up to lines 17 and 18 to see how the methods are invoked. We take our instance of the structure that we named `myTn` and simply use the dot operator to invoke the methods, just as if they were fields. This is different from what you might be familiar with if you're coming from a language like C++ or Java. Go does not have classes, and the methods (also called member functions in C++) in Go are not inside of the structure. The association between method and type is established by the receiver.

6.2   Custom Packages and Visibility

In this book, we've used some packages that are available as part of Go's libraries. But you can create your own custom packages, too.

For a package that Go provides, you have simply used code such as:

```
import(
    "fmt"
)
```

But, if we make a custom package, we can explicitly describe where the package is located, such as:

```
import(
    "./pack1/pack1"
)
```

In the above case, the `pack1` package is available in a directory inside the same directory in which the importing source file resides. In other words, if we have one file called `packageTest.go` that imports `pack1`, we would have a `pack1` directory inside the same directory as `packageTest.go`.

And, as another note, we must resolve the name using the dot operator, just like with the built-in Go libraries. For example, we use `fmt.Printf()` to resolve the `Printf()` function available from the `fmt` package. Similarly, we would use `pack1.FunctionName()` to import a function from `pack1`.

6.2.1   Visibility

The first topic we must consider when dealing with packages is *visibility*. Visibility refers to the ability of a function, method, or data to be accessed from outside a package. This is similar to the concept of `public` and `private` data members and member functions/methods in languages like C++ and Java. When an identifier is available outside of a package, it is said to be *exported*.

Go has a very unique approach to indicate whether data or functions are exported or not. Instead of a particular keyword, Go uses the case of the identifier.

143

If an identifier in a package is uppercase, then the identifier is exported, and therefore available outside of the package. If the identifier is lowercase, it is not exported.

Let's look at an example. Keep in mind that this time we have two different source files to consider. One will be the package we are creating, and the other is the *driver* program, which means the program that utilizes the package.

Firstly, we must create a package. While not entirely necessary, it is good to make a directory to put the package source file in (which will be compiled into an object file). In my case, I call the directory the same name as the package, namely, `pack1`.

Here is the code for the package. Note the location given is not part of the code:

(Location : pack1/pack1.go)

```
1  package pack1
2
3  var MyPack1Int int = 15;
4
5  func ReturnNum() int{
6    return 5;
7  }
```

The package code is fairly self-explanatory. The only thing that is really different is on line 1. Notice the package name is not `main`. Instead, we named this package `pack1`. This is the name that will be imported in the driver program.

Now, here is the code for the driver program:

(Location : packageTest.go)

```
1
2    package main
3
4    import(
5      "fmt"
6      "./pack1/pack1"
7    )
8
9    func main(){
10     var test1 int;
11
12     test1 = pack1.ReturnNum();
13     fmt.Printf("Hi there\n");
14     fmt.Printf("Num : %d\n", test1);
15
16     fmt.Printf("Num 2 : %d\n", pack1.MyPack1Int);
17   }
```

Here is the output:

```
johnbaugh@ubuntu:~/Desktop/go_programming/chap6/packages$ .
/6.out
Hi there
Num : 5
Num 2 : 15
```

Again, once you understand what's going on here, we can
see that the code is not that difficult. Notice how the
package is imported on line 6. We specify the directory
and package name as we saw earlier.

When we want to call the function ReturnNum(), we
qualify it with the name of the package, pack1 and use the
dot operator to qualify it as we can see on line 12.

Again, we can access data from our custom package just as
well as we accessed our function, just as long as the name
begins with an uppercase letter. So, we can access
MyPack1Int on line 16.

Before we move on, it's important to note that you must compile the pack1.go source file before you compile the packageTest.go driver source file. The driver is actually looking for pack1.6, the compiled object code. That is why it must be available, or the driver will not compile.

Since we learned about structs previously, it would be important that we note you can create and utilize exported structures as well. Let's consider some more code:

(Location : structPack.go)

```
1   package structPack
2
3   type ExportedStruct struct{
4     Member1 int;
5     Member2 float;
6   }
```

(Location : main.go)

```
1    package main
2    import(
3      "fmt"
4      "./structPack"
5    )
6
7    func main(){
8      var myStruct *structPack.ExportedStruct;
9      myStruct = new(structPack.ExportedStruct);
10
11     myStruct.Member1 = 10;
12     myStruct.Member2 = 16.0;
13
14     fmt.Printf("Member1 = %d\n", myStruct.Member1);
15     fmt.Printf("Member2 = %f\n", myStruct.Member2);
16   }
```

And the output is:

```
johnbaugh@ubuntu:~/Desktop/go_programming/chap6/package2$ .
/6.out
Member1 = 10
Member2 = 16.000000
```

This example is also fairly clear if you understood the previous example. In the above example, take note that the name of the structure itself, `ExportedStruct` is capitalized. Also, the members that we access are also capitalized, namely, `Member1` and `Member2`. If there was a member that began with a lowercase character, we could not access it from outside of the package. Additionally, if we had a struct type whose name began with a lowercase letter, we could not declare an instance of the struct type itself.

6.3   Interfaces

An *interface* defines a set of methods, called the *method set*. Interfaces are pure and abstract. This means that they don't have implementations or data fields. Another concept is that of *interface types*. Interface types are any type that implements the interface.

This means that the type has methods that are a subset (proper or not) of the interface. As long as the type has methods that are *at least* the methods in the method set of the interface, then this qualifies that type as implementing the interface.

Finally, an *interface value* is an actual value with its type being the interface type. It will be more clear once we examine some examples, but for now, we must establish that multiple types could implement the same interface. An interface type can point to an instance of any of the types that implements the interface. This allows for great flexibility.

As with most topics in this book, examples are the best way to give us a stronger grasp on the concepts of an interface.

Let's see some code:

```
1    package main
2    import(
3       "fmt"
4    )
5
6    type Square struct{
7       sideLength int;
8    }
9
10   type Triangle struct{
11      base int;
12      height int;
13   }
14
15   type AreaInterface interface{
16      Area() float;
17   }
18
19   func main(){
20      var mySquare *Square;
21      var myTriangle *Triangle;
22      var areaInt AreaInterface;
23
24      mySquare = new(Square);
25      myTriangle = new(Triangle);
26
27      mySquare.sideLength = 5;
28      myTriangle.base = 3;
29      myTriangle.height = 5;
30
31      areaInt = mySquare;
32      fmt.Printf("The square has area : %f\n",
     areaInt.Area());
33
34      areaInt = myTriangle;
35      fmt.Printf("The triangle has area : %f\n",
     areaInt.Area());
36
37   }
38
39   // Square implements the AreaInterface interface
40   func (sq *Square) Area() float{
41      return float(sq.sideLength * sq.sideLength);
42   }
43
```

```
44   // Triangle implements the AreaInterface interface
45   func (tr *Triangle) Area() float{
46     return 0.5 * float(tr.base * tr.height);
47   }
```

And here's the output:

```
johnbaugh@ubuntu:~/Desktop/go_programming/chap6/interface1$
./6.out
The square has area : 25.000000
The triangle has area : 7.500000
```

This program has a lot going on. It combines a lot of the things we've learned throughout the book, as well as interface types, which we just learned in this section. In fact, it is one of the largest programs we've looked at in this book thus far.

On lines 6 - 13, we declare two different structure types, Square and Triangle. Square has a sideLength field, which is the measurement of a square's side. In Triangle, there are two fields, base and height, indicating the length of the base and the height of the triangle. In other words, we have the data that is required to determine the area of either a Square or a Triangle.

On lines 15 - 17, we declare our interface type, AreaInterface. The interface has only one method, Area() that returns a float. In other for a type to implement this interface, it must only implement the Area() method.

On lines 20 - 22, we declare our Square and Triangle structure types, as well as our AreaInterface type. On lines 24 and 25, we actually create our Square and Triangle, mySquare and myTriangle, respectively using new(). And then, on lines 27-29, we set the values of the sideLength of our Square and the base and height of our Triangle.

On lines 31 and 32 are where the really interesting and new stuff happens. On line 31, we assign the `Square` variable to our interface variable, `areaInt`. This interface variable now contains a reference to the `Square` variable. We can then call `areaInt.Area()`. This actually calls the `Area()` method of `Square`, which is defined on 40-42.

Later, on lines 34 and 35, we store our `Triangle` variable into `areaInt`. And, although we call the exact same method, `Area()`, what is actually called is the `Area()` method of `Triangle`, defined on lines 44-47.

This is all possible because an interface variable can contain a reference of any type that implements its method set. Since both `Square` and `Triangle` implement the `Area()` method (the only method in the method set of `AreaInterface`), an `AreaInterface` variable can contain either a `Square` or a `Triangle`.

This is the closest thing to polymorphism that Go has. And, while `areaInt` does contain a reference to either the `Square` or `Triangle` variable (pointer variable, to be exact), the `areaInt` is not a pointer itself. It is a multiword data structure, containing the value of the receiver (which could be a pointer, or a variable of the type itself) and a method table pointer that points to the appropriate method. For example, when `areaInt` refers to a `Square`, it maintains both the field data and value of the `Square` variable, as well as the appropriate `Area()` method, namely, the `Square`'s `Area()` method.

6.4   Summary

In the first part of this chapter, we learned about structured types. We learned about named and anonymous fields of these structured types. Also, we learned about how to implement special functions, called methods, that act upon these structured types.

We also learned about how to create our own custom packages. Along with packages, we learned about visibility and how the case of the first character of identifiers within a package determines whether or not the identifier can be accessed outside the package.

Finally, we discussed interfaces. We learned that interfaces allow us to describe a set of methods that define the interface, and how a type must implement each of these methods in order to qualify as implementing that particular interface. We also learned that an interface type allows us to store a variable or reference to any of its implementing types. This is similar to the concept of polymorphism present in all fully object oriented languages, although not exactly the same.

Chapter 7

Concurrency and Communication Channels

In this chapter we will discuss slightly more complicated features of Go. Go comes with built-in types and functionality to help with concurrency and communication. This chapter reveals much of the interesting characteristics of Go that make it a superb language for modern computing paradigms.

7.1   Concurrency

In this section, we will discuss how Go handles *concurrency*. Concurrency allows programs, processes, threads, and in the case of Go, *goroutines* (more on these later) to operate simultaneously. Sometimes these entities share resources as well, so this sharing must be coordinated properly. Go offers a lot of support for concurrency and makes resource sharing and coordination between such simultaneously executing entities. In order to understand exactly how does this, we must explore goroutines.

7.1.1 Goroutines

Typically, when talking about concurrency (also called *parallelization*), you will almost certainly hear two terms: *process* and *thread*. While these terms are often confused, and there are some individuals who split hairs over details, basically a *process* is an independently executing entity that runs in its own address space. Composing a process may be one or more *threads*, which are simultaneously executing entities that share address space.

With Go, the designers wanted to avoid confusion or preconceptions (and especially, the hair-splitting over details), so they named their parallelization entities *goroutines*. A goroutine is essentially a thread, which shares address space with other goroutines within the same process.

A goroutine is implemented as a function, and invoked (called) with the go keyword.

A code sample follows:

```
1    package main;
2
3    import(
4      "fmt"
5      "time"
6    )
7
8    func main(){
9
10     fmt.Println("In main()");
11     go longWait();
12     go shortWait();
13     fmt.Println("About to sleep in  main()");
14     time.Sleep(10 * 1e9);
15     fmt.Println("At the end of main()");
16   }
17
18   func longWait(){
```

153

```
19    fmt.Println("Beginning longWait()");
20    time.Sleep(5 * 1e9); //sleep for 5 seconds 5 *
      1,000,000,000ns
21    fmt.Println("End of longWait()");
22  }
23
24  func shortWait(){
25    fmt.Println("Beginning shortWait()");
26    time.Sleep(2 * 1e9);
27    fmt.Println("End of shortWait()");
28  }
```

And the output is:

```
johnbaugh@ubuntu:~/Desktop/go_programming/chap7/goroutine$
./6.out
In main()
About to sleep in  main()
Beginning longWait()
Beginning shortWait()
End of shortWait()
End of longWait()
At the end of main()
```

Before we discuss the goroutines themselves, notice we have included the `time` package. We need this in order to use the `Sleep()` method. `Sleep()` has the following signature:

```
 func Sleep(ns int64) os.Error{
//function body here
}
```

Note that we could capture an error (the return type) if we wish. The parameter is in *nanoseconds*, which means billionths of a second. The `Sleep()` method allows us to pause the current goroutine for at least a certain number of nanoseconds.

In our code, notice that in both `longWait()` and `shortWait()`, we have a multiplication by `1e9`. What does this mean? This means 1 times 10 to the power 9, in other words, a 1 followed by 9 zeroes. We do this multiplication to get seconds. Since a nanosecond is one billionth of a second, we need to multiply a nanosecond by a billion (1,000,000,000) to get one second. So any number we have multiplied by 1e9 will give us the number of seconds.

On lines 11 and 12, we use the go keyword to start the goroutines. When you execute the code, you will notice that each of these functions will start independently and not end in the same order that you would expect if they were typical functions.

The function shortWait() sleeps for 2 seconds, while longWait() sleeps for 5. I have the main function sleep for 10 to ensure that it doesn't exit before the two goroutines do.

Much of the magic of this program will be evident when you run the program. I cannot, on this statically printed paper (or digitally typed data file, more accurately) accurately express the dynamics of this code. You will have to run it and see that it does in fact wait after the two "beginning" statements are printed. Note that the "End of shortWait()" string is printed before the "End of longWait()" string.

This was a very basic and trivial example just so you can see what can be done with goroutines. We will explore more of their power later in this chapter.

7.2   Communication Channels

Related to goroutines are communication channels, a built-in reference type that provide mechanisms to perform cross-goroutine communication. Goroutines must be able to communicate in order to send and receive information and coordinate their efforts.

The keyword for a channel is `chan`. Since channels are reference types, you must use the `make()` function to allocate memory for them.

Channels are specified with the data type that transmit. Thus, the generic form:

```
chan data_type;
```

declares a channel that allows for sending and receiving of `data_type` data.

Specifically, if I want to transmit, say, integer data, I could create a channel thusly:

```
chan int;
```

7.2.1   The Communication Operator, <-

We use the *communication operator*, `<-` to designate that we are transmitting data. The data is transmitted in the direction of the arrow. For example,

```
myInt = <- ch;
```

would indicate that `myInt` is receiving the data from a channel, `ch`. The data is flowing *from* the channel, *to* the integer variable. However,

```
ch <- someInt;
```

would indicate that `someInt` is being sent over the channel, `ch`.

Let's look at a fairly simple, "quick and dirty" example of how to use channels. Note that this is not an excellent implementation, and that we will explore better examples later. But for now, it will get the point across without unnecessary difficulty:

```
1    package main;
2    import(
3      "fmt"
4      "time"
5    )
6
7    func main(){
8      var ch chan string;
9
10     ch = make(chan string);
11
12     go sendData(ch);
13     go getData(ch);
14
15     time.Sleep(3 * 1e9);
16   }
17
18   func sendData(ch chan string){
19       ch <- "John";
20       ch <- "Bob";
21       ch <- "Sam";
22       ch <- "Sally";
23       ch <- "Julie";
24   }
25
26   func getData(ch chan string){
27     var input string;
28
29     for{
30       input = <- ch;
31       fmt.Printf("%s\n", input);
32     }
33   }
```

And the output is:

157

```
johnbaugh@ubuntu:~/Desktop/go_programming/chap7/namepump$ .
/6.out
John
Bob
Sam
Sally
Julie
```

In this code, we declare and initialize our channel of strings, ch, on lines 8-10. We then call two functions (in this case, they are goroutines), sendData() and getData(), passing ch to them in order to provide a mechanism for communication between them.

If we skip down a little bit in the code, and look at lines 18-24, we see the body of sendData(). Since our channel is a channel that utilizes strings, we are able to send various strings across it. In this case, we've used some names.

On the other side of the channel, we have our receiver goroutine on lines 26-32, called getData(). Notice that we have an infinite for loop that has within its body, a string variable input being set to whatever comes out of the channel, and then we print the data. The reason it will eventually break is that when the channel is closed (when the channel goes out of scope in the sendData() function), the for loop will exit.

Let's hop back up into the main function for a bit, on line 15. Note that right now, we are using a little quick and dirty trick to keep the program from terminating before the goroutines have a chance to execute. Specifically, we are sleeping for 3 seconds. This gives us enough time for the goroutines to send and receive data, respectively. If you run the code, you will notice that even after the data is done being sent and received (and in our case, printed), the program doesn't terminate until three seconds have elapsed.

158

Our above approach is a little naïve and clunky. How can we make it better? Well, we must first consider what causes us to exit the `main()` function in the first place. Since we call `go` on both of our functions (lines 12 and 13), the `main()` method has nothing to do except exit, unless we put the `Sleep()` function at the end to keep it from finishing.

Why don't we just call the second function, `getData()` instead of causing it to execute in its own goroutine?

Well, if you simply do this, you will end up with a runtime error. The system will detect a potential deadlock. Is there any way we could signal when we are done with the channel on the `sendData()` side, and is there any way to detect that the channel is closed on the `getData()` side? In fact, there are.

The method

```
close(ch);
```

closes a channel, `ch`. The method

```
closed(ch);
```

returns `true` if the channel is closed, and `false` if it isn't.

Let's look at the code in total with some of our old code commented out, and new code added.

The output will be the same, except we don't have to wait at the end of `main()`, because there is no `Sleep()` method.

```
1    package main;
2    import(
3      "fmt"
4    //   "time"
```

```
5     )
6
7     func main(){
8        var ch chan string;
9
10       ch = make(chan string);
11
12       go sendData(ch);
13    //   go getData(ch);
14       getData(ch);
15
16    //   time.Sleep(3 * 1e9);
17    }
18
19    func sendData(ch chan string){
20       ch <- "John";
21       ch <- "Bob";
22       ch <- "Sam";
23       ch <- "Sally";
24       ch <- "Julie";
25       close(ch);
26    }
27
28    func getData(ch chan string){
29       var input string;
30
31       for{
32          input = <- ch;
33          if(closed(ch)){
34             break;
35          }
36          fmt.Printf("%s\n", input);
37       }
38    }
```

Here, we have call sendData() with go on line 12 just as the original code. On line 14, we simply call the function without go this time. This will prevent the program from exiting too early, since this function will share the main process (or main goroutine if you wish).

The changes to the functions themselves should be apparent. On line 25, we've added the close() function to send a message that the channel is finished sending data. And, on lines 33-35, the condition of the channel is tested. If the channel is closed, we break outside of the loop.

7.2.2   Communicability and Select Statements

There are situations in which we may want to know if the channel has blocked or not. Go does provide a way to do this.
If we want to know if a receive on a channel has blocked or not, we can use the following syntax:

```
value, proceed = <-chan;
```

In this case, `value` is the value received on the channel and `proceed` is a Boolean value that is set to `true` if we have received the value.

For sending, in a similar fashion we can collect the value:

```
proceed := chan <- value;
```

We can use this with a conditional statement in order to see if we can proceed.

Go provides a very special conditional construct just for communication channels, the `select` statement. The `select` statement is essentially a `switch` statement, but for use exclusively with control channels. Thus, each case must be either a send or receive communication.

Let's consider a code sample:

```
1    package main
2    import(
3      "fmt"
4      "time"
5    )
6
```

```
7   func main(){
8     var ch1 chan int;   //chan of ints
9     var ch2 chan int;   //chan of ints
10
11    ch1 = make(chan int);
12    ch2 = make(chan int);
13
14    go pump1(ch1);
15    go pump2(ch2);
16    go suck(ch1, ch2);
17
18    time.Sleep(10 * 1e9);
19  }
20
21  func pump1(ch chan int){
22    for i:= 0; ; i++{
23    ch <-i*2;
24    }
25  }
26
27  func pump2(ch chan int){
28    for i:=0; ; i++{
29    ch <- i+5;
30    }
31  }
32
33  func suck(ch1 chan int, ch2 chan int){
34    for{
35      select{
36      case v:= <-ch1:
37        fmt.Printf("Received on channel 1 : %d\n", v);
38      case v:= <-ch2:
39        fmt.Printf("Received on channel 2 : %d\n", v);
40      }
41    }
42  }
```

I won't put the output here, because it is extensive, and will likely (in fact, almost certainly) be different when you execute it, even between multiple runs of the same program on the same machine. Additionally, the output will be quite long. You can decrease the amount of output by decreasing the amount of time the program sleeps for.

You will undoubtedly notice that the output will alternate between receiving on channel 1 and channel 2. There are two pumps, producing integers and sending them on their respective channels. Only one consumer (the `suck()` function) is present, which takes the information on either of the channels, and prints the information out. Notice that it is in an infinite for loop, polling for information being sent over the channels.

The `select` statement switches on the information received on the channels. The `case` that is chosen is dependent upon which channel the information is received.

7.3   A Simple Client and Server

In this section, we will explore a simple client/server application. In this application, the client will specify its name, and then send information to the server.

The code for the server should be in its own source code file, such as `server.go`, and is as follows:

```
1    package main
2
3    import(
4      "fmt"
5      "net"
6      "os"
7    )
8
9    func main(){
10     var listener net.Listener;
11     var error os.Error;
12     var conn net.Conn;
13
14     fmt.Printf("Starting the server...\n");
15
16     //create listener
17     listener, error = net.Listen("tcp",
     "localhost:50000");
18     if error != nil{
19       fmt.Println("Error listening", error.String());
```

163

```
20        return; //terminate program.
21      }//end if error != nil
22
23      //listen and accept connections from clients
24      for{
25        conn, error = listener.Accept();
26        if error != nil{
27          fmt.Println("Error accepting", error.String());
28          return;  //terminate program
29        }//end if error != nil
30
31        go doServerStuff(conn);   //do something with this
     connection
32      }//end for
33    }
34
35    func doServerStuff(conn net.Conn){
36
37      var buf []byte;
38      var error os.Error;
39
40      for{
41        buf = make([]byte, 512);
42        _, error = conn.Read(buf);
43        if error != nil{
44          return;
45        }
46
47        fmt.Printf("Received data : %v", string(buf));
48      }//end for
49    }
```

In the code for the server, we will use a package we are
unfamiliar with. This package, net, has many capabilities
to aid in sockets, and other network communication
functionality. It contains capabilities to aid with TCP/IP,
UDP, domain name resolution, and more.

The variable listener of type net.Listener, declared on
line 10 is used to listen for incoming communication from
clients. Notice on line 17, it is instantiated to listen on TCP
port 50,000 on localhost.

On line 12, conn of type net.Conn is instantiated on line
25 where the actual connection is created from the listener.

164

The main goroutine of the server waits on incoming connections on line 25 inside of the infinite `for` loop, and then continues once it receives information from the listener. If there are no errors, the program goes to line 32 where a separate goroutine is created for that client. So each client gets its own goroutine. The function `doServerStuff(conn net.Conn)` is the goroutine that is called.

Lines 35-50 show the definition for our goroutine, `doServerStuff()`. We create a buffer called `buf`, of the type `byte` slice. The buffer is instantiated with 512 bytes of memory on line 41, then waits and reads information into the buffer on line 42. If there are no errors, the information from the client is printed out on the server side (line 47). Notice that the buffer is cast explicitly to a `string`.

Now, the code for the client, which should be in its own code file, say `client.go`, is as follows:

```
1    package main
2    import(
3      "fmt"
4      "net"
5      "os"
6      "bufio"
7      "strings"
8    )
9
10   //CLIENT
11   func main(){
12     var conn net.Conn;
13     var error os.Error;
14     var inputReader *bufio.Reader;
15     var input string;
16     var clientName string;
17
18     conn,error = net.Dial("tcp","","localhost:50000");
19     if error != nil{
20       fmt.Printf("Error : ", error.String());
21       return;
22     }//end if
```

```
23
24        inputReader = bufio.NewReader(os.Stdin);
25
26        fmt.Println("First, what is your name?\n");
27
28        clientName,_ = inputReader.ReadString('\n');
29        trimmedClient := strings.Trim(clientName, "\n");
30
31        for{
32        fmt.Println("What to send to the server?  Type Q to
    quit.");
33        input,_ = inputReader.ReadString('\n');
34
35        trimmedInput := strings.Trim(input, "\n");
36        if(trimmedInput == "Q"){
37            return;
38        }
39
40        _, error = conn.Write([]byte(trimmedClient + "
    says: " + input));
41        }
42  }
```

For the client code, we must include the net package for
network communication as well as the bufio package, for
getting input from the user. The client doesn't need a
listener like the server does. Instead, on line 18, it dials the
server on TCP port 50,000. If you don't start the server
first (or if other problems exist), an error will be printed out
on line 20.

If there are no errors, we create an input reader to obtain
information from standard input, on line 24. The user is
prompted to enter their name, which they should do on line
28. We then have to perform a trim to remove the newline
character that the user enters. This is so the information
sent to the server doesn't have an unnecessary newline
character inside of it.

Later, in lines 31-41, the user can enter information to send
to the server. If they type a single character Q, the client
exits.

Notice on line 40, the information that is actually sent to the server. It prepends the data with the name of the user (that they typed right after starting the client application) and the string, "says". This is so if there are several clients communicating with the server (which we encourage you to try) the server side console will show which client said what.

The server must be started first, before the client. The server output is as follows:

```
johnbaugh@ubuntu:~/Desktop/go_programming/simple_IM/server$
./6.out
Starting the server...
Received data : John says: Hi there
Received data : John says: This is the client
```

On the client side, the interaction looks like this:

```
johnbaugh@ubuntu:~/Desktop/go_programming/simple_IM/client$
./6.out
First, what is your name?

John
What to send to the server?  Type Q to quit.
Hi there
What to send to the server?  Type Q to quit.
This is the client
What to send to the server?  Type Q to quit.
```

You will have two console windows (or tabs) opened at once. In my particular implementation, I put the client and server code in separate subdirectories. I compile them separately. Then, I start the server first, and then the client.

After starting the server, you can start several clients and send information to the server.

I encourage the reader to modify the server and to play around with this basic code.

Ideas for modifying the code:

- Determine a way to send information to the server, perhaps the message "shutdown" and have the server exit
- Determine a way to track the users that log in, on server side and then add another command to the available commands, "who" which returns a list of the names of all connected clients.
- Create a program using some of what you learned in order to have the server forward information to other clients that you pick. In other words, it would be like a simple instant messaging program.

There are endless possibilities. The information in this chapter was quite simple, but should give you a basic idea of how the `net` package works. As always, to read more about this package and its thorough documentation, you can go to the official Go Language site (*http://www.golang.org*).

7.4　　Summary

In this chapter, we studied concurrency and communication channels. I introduced *goroutines*, which are similar to threads and used for concurrency in Go. We then discussed communication channels, which allows for communication between goroutines. This significantly reduces the traditional resource accessing problems found in many other languages when dealing with cross-thread communication. Finally, we put much of our knowledge together and created a simple, yet complete, client-server application.

Conclusion and Further Study

Go is a very powerful language. In this book, we have explored the fundamentals of the Go programming language. This book is by no means exhaustive, however, and you need to know that there are dozens of packages available with Go. In order to explore these packages, visit the official Go Programming site at:

http://www.golang.org

This book has been edited and corrections have been made. We've attempted to ensure the highest possible quality, but it is rare when a technical book is printed without any errors or at least some need for clarification. Thus, if and when any errata are discovered, they will be corrected at this book's official site:

http://www.goprogrammingbook.com

You will also be able to submit questions, requests for clarifications, and errata on this site. Also, check out the site for further information, clarifications, news, and source code samples.

Index